Baby Sussex

By royal correspondent
Robert Jobson

ISBN: 978-1-906670-86-3

About the author

Robert Jobson is a best-selling and award-winning author and royal correspondent who has chronicled the story of the House of Windsor for the past 30 years, and is internationally recognised for his in-depth and historical knowledge of the Royal Family. In addition to making regular appearances as an on-screen expert for Sky News, the BBC, ITV and Channel 5, Robert is Royal Editor of the *London Evening Standard* in the UK; Royal Contributor for NBC's *Today Show* and *Forbes* magazine in the US; and is a regular on national television in Australia and New Zealand.

Contents

Introduction

The Duke and Duchess of Sussex's historic decision to step back from their roles as senior royals and establish a new life together in North America has threatened to rock the institution of monarchy to its foundations.

Until that point, every move they made – from their courtship, culminating in a spectacular wedding in May 2018 to the birth of their son, Archie, a year later – seemed to dominate the headlines. They had become the new star couple in the Royal Family, popular and feted wherever they went. But behind the beaming smiles they were struggling to cope with the demands of public duty and the relentless scrutiny it placed them under. We now know they were feeling tormented by the conflicting forces of the weight of public expectation put upon them and their own personal prospects of future happiness.

Towards the end of 2019, Harry embarked on secret talks with the Queen and the Prince of Wales, which focused on how he saw the future for his family. It was, almost inevitably, at odds with the more traditional values of his grandmother and father, which placed royal duty above everything. After all, the Queen and Prince Charles had been raised from childhood with the heavy burden of being first in line to the throne. In their lives, public service always came before their personal hopes and dreams. Harry, whose life had been made complete by marriage to the woman he loved and the birth of their first child, wanted something very different for himself and his family.

Having slipped down to sixth in line to the throne, following the birth of his brother Prince William's three children, Harry knew he would never be King. Instead, he had hoped to carve out a new, more self-funding,

"progressive role" where he and his family could live overseas some of the time but still have a "part-time" position inside the Royal Family. They would be royals, just not senior royals; and they would still serve, just not all of the time.

However, the Queen and Prince Charles did not agree with the Sussexes' future template. And it was they, not Harry and Meghan, who would call the shots. After many weeks of secret discussions that dragged on into January, the Sussexes were bounced into going public when their plans were leaked. They went ahead and issued a statement, despite the Queen expressly asking them to keep all discussions under wraps until a compromise could be found.

There followed weeks of discussions and behind-the-scenes wrangling. In the end, Her Majesty came down on the side of preserving the reputation of the monarchy over peace and harmony within her family. She effectively stopped Harry and Meghan from using their HRH titles for commercial enterprises and ruled that there were no half measures when it came to being royal, senior or otherwise. The Queen must have told Harry and Meghan that they had to be all in or all out... and that was it. They were out of The Firm.

Her Majesty ruled that while the Sussexes would always be beloved members of her family, their being part-time royals couldn't work. She also insisted that the £2.5 million the taxpayer put towards their UK property – Frogmore Cottage in Windsor – would have to be paid back and they would no longer receive money from the Sovereign Grant. Harry also lost his military patronages, such as his prized position as Captain General of the Royal Marines. Moreover, the Sussexes would not be permitted to trade under the name Sussex Royal. This was a significant setback as they had already registered companies and operated their online media platforms – an official website and an Instagram page with 11.2 million followers – using the brand name.

The Sussexes, who over Christmas 2019 had spent an extended holiday in Canada mulling over their future, initially decided to resettle there. Although they had failed to get The Firm to agree to the roles they ideally wanted, the pair accepted their new position with good grace. Having subsequently chosen to set up home in the US in California, Harry and Meghan can now live the life they have dreamed of, away from media intrusion. Archie's childhood will be a far cry from the one Harry experienced, lived out in the glare of TV and newspaper spotlights.

From their new base, the Sussexes have started to develop commercial and charitable activities. These will enable them to finance their own lives and to develop as global philanthropists. More importantly, they can develop their new roles with a better work–life balance than they could ever have hoped possible, with the relative privacy they have always craved.

Harry has admitted he felt he had no choice but to step away as a senior royal. Nonetheless, he promised at a charity dinner for his HIV/AIDS charity Sentebale that he and Meghan were not just walking away. "The decision that I have made for my wife and I to step back is not one I made lightly," he said. "It was so many months of talks after so many years of challenges and I know I haven't always gotten it right but as far as this goes there really was no other option."

Friends of the couple say they are now blissfully happy with their new life and do not regret the seemingly earth-shattering decision to step back from their royal roles. The Sussexes will be coming back and spending time in the UK going forward. Only time will tell if they realise their hopes and dreams, but I, like so many, wish them both well and hope they find the peace, privacy and stability they desire as a family.

Robert Jobson

Chapter one

THE NEW
FAMILY SUSSEX

Expecting great things

Harry and Meghan's excitement about the prospect of pregnancy was in evidence long before any changes in the duchess's appearance

The Duke and Duchess of Sussex made no secret of their desire to start a family and even addressed the idea of having children in their engagement interview. When asked if they had plans to try for a baby, Prince Harry replied: "Not currently, no," garnering a laugh from Meghan, seated next to him. He went on, "Of course, one step at a time and hopefully we'll start a family in the near future."

Around the time Meghan met Harry in the spring of 2016, she gave an interview in which she said becoming a mother was "on her bucket list". She said, "I can't wait to start a family, but in due time." A few months later Meghan went further in *Lifestyle* magazine. "I also dream to have a family. It's all about balance, and I have so much happiness in my career and am fortunate to travel the world and see so many amazing things – it will also be nice to be anchored to something grounded and in the same place. Raising a family will be a wonderful part of that."

Meghan's estranged father, Thomas Markle, said in an interview on *Good Morning Britain*: "She's wanted children for a long time. When she met Harry and she spoke about how much she loved him, [I thought] there's got to be a child in the making there somewhere soon." Her former agent Gina Nelthorpe-Cowne also said in an interview: "Meghan said to me, 'I would absolutely love to have children, and I can't wait to be a mother'."

Much was made too of Meghan lingering at a baby products stand during an official visit to Northern Ireland prior to the royal wedding in April 2018 and saying, "I'm sure at some point we'll need the whole thing." She was also photographed crouching down talking to a little girl at the Coworth Polo Club in Ascot in July 2018 at around the time the couple are thought to have conceived.

Harry had been broody for years. He said in a 2010 interview when he was just 25, "I'm obsessed with children." He also spoke of his desire to settle down during a tour of New Zealand in 2015. Then aged 30, he said he was waiting for the right moment – and the right woman – to come along. "Of course, I would love to have kids right now," he said. "But there's a process that one has to go through."

Happily, that process started quite soon afterwards when he announced his engagement to Meghan. And since Harry's bride-to-be was older than him, everyone assumed the couple would crack on with the business of trying for a baby once they'd tied the knot.

In early August 2018, which must have been around the time Meghan conceived, she attended the wedding of Harry's close friends, Charlie van Straubenzee and Daisy Jenks, in Surrey. Her petite frame looked chic in a black sleeveless blouse tucked into a floaty pleated midi-skirt by Club Monaco. The following month in September,

she looked sensational in a long-sleeved black dress by Givenchy, which featured a thigh-high slit and fitted bodice. Rather than hiding a baby bump, she drew attention to her slim waist with a gold and black belt.

By early October, speculation that she was pregnant was rife. Yet the duchess stepped out in a tight leather pencil skirt. The royals were visiting Sussex and for the day trip, Meghan chose a Hugo Boss number that skimmed over her very tiny bump.

On 12 October, Meghan attended Princess Eugenie's wedding in an elegant, double-breasted blue Givenchy coat. Of the five pairs of buttons on the garment, the bottom three were left undone. This sparked more definite speculation among royal watchers that the duchess was pregnant. Subsequently, it emerged that this had been the day that a beaming Harry and Meghan had announced their impending parenthood to the rest of the family.

On 15 October 2018, as the Sussexes arrived in Australia at the start of their Commonwealth tour, the Palace made the announcement that they were expecting their first child. Kensington Palace said the couple, who had wed in Windsor five months earlier, were "delighted to be able to share this happy news with the public". Meghan's mother, Doria Ragland, issued a sweet statement through Kensington Palace about her daughter's news, saying she is "very happy at this lovely news and is looking forward to welcoming her first grandchild." The Palace declined to comment on whether Meghan's father, Thomas Markle, had been told. It later emerged that there was no contact between father and daughter.

Previous pages: Harry and Meghan make an entrance at the Endeavour Fund Awards, February 2019

Above: The newly expectant couple take a walk during their tour of Australia, October 2018

Opposite: Prince Harry gives his wife a loving look, October 2018

The duke and duchess, pictured during a walkabout in New Zealand, October 2018

A few weeks later, Meghan's bump had started to show and, indeed, she no longer needed to hide her pregnancy as the couple had already confirmed their exciting news. Meghan's changing figure was clear to see in the first week of her Australia tour, when she sported a navy Dion Lee dress that showed off her new curves. After that – and throughout her pregnancy – the duchess proudly showed off her baby bump and happily chatted to the public about how she felt.

During a walkabout on Fraser Island, Meghan's hand rested on her barely visible bump as she greeted well-wishers. The mum-to-be wore a floaty striped linen dress by American eco-friendly brand Reformation, which perfectly complimented her changing figure. A few days later she looked sensational at a reception and state dinner hosted by the President of Fiji, this time subtly shrouding her blossoming bump in a full-length, cornflower blue caped gown by designer Safiyaa.

"The duchess proudly showed off her baby bump and happily chatted to the public about how she felt"

The duchess's bump really started to show in November. Meghan was pictured arriving at the Royal Variety Performance in London – her first time at the event, where she accompanied Harry. She looked stunning in a black halter-neck top with white floral embroidery, again by Safiyaa, and an elegant floor-length black skirt. Her bump was also visible when she visited Zaheera Sufyaan at the Hubb Community Kitchen in west London.

In early December the duke and duchess stepped out for a charity carol service alongside some of Harry's closest friends. This time Meghan, who showed her support for the cause by reading a beautiful poem at the service, was not photographed by the press but was thought to be wearing a Seraphine maternity dress. At this stage she had not been seen out in public for weeks, so fans were delighted to get an update on baby Sussex.

The mother-to-be made a surprise appearance at the British Fashion Awards on 10 December, where she was reunited with her wedding dress designer Clare Waight Keller. Dressed in another show-stopping black Givenchy gown – this time a sleek, one-shouldered, floor-length number – Meghan cradled her baby bump as she presented Waight Keller with the prestigious British Womenswear Designer of the Year Award. The crowd went wild.

Opposite: Meghan and her baby bump make a special appearance at the Fashion Awards 2018

On 18 December, during a visit to the Royal Variety Charity's Brinsworth House in Twickenham, Meghan laughed as she told one of the residents, "I'm feeling very pregnant today". It's true that her high-yoked, white Brock Collection floral dress with short sleeves hugged – and seemed to emphasise – her burgeoning bump. She covered up outside with a grey wool Soia & Kyo coat, its belt tied casually just under the bust.

On 25 December the duchess's bump made another public appearance when she and the Duke of Sussex joined the Royal Family at the church in Sandringham for their traditional Christmas Day service. Wearing a chic navy Victoria Beckham coat, Meghan kept herself and baby warm as she walked arm-in-arm with the beaming dad-to-be, her husband Prince Harry. The duchess never gave an exact due date for her first baby, but fans were hugely excited when she told members of the crowd outside, "Nearly there!" when they asked about the baby.

In January 2019, Meghan visited the Mayhew animal welfare charity in Kensal Rise, west London, wearing an Emporio Armani cashmere overcoat, an H&M maternity dress and toting a vegan leather Stella McCartney bag. She charmed staff by cuddling a Jack Russell called Minnie and sharing anecdotes about her own dogs, including a beagle who had come from a rescue centre in Toronto. Meghan also visited another charity close to her heart, Smart Works in nearby Ladbroke Grove, which helps long-term unemployed women regain the skills and confidence to return to employment.

Right: Harry and Meghan visit the Royal Moroccan Equestrian Federation, February 2019

The new family Sussex

Opposite: The Duke and Duchess of Sussex attend a Commonwealth Day youth event, March 2019

Below: Meghan, on the last public engagement of her pregnancy, and Harry pay tribute to the victims of the Christchurch mosque attack, March 2019

In February, Harry and Meghan made a stylish couple at the Endeavour Fund Awards at London's Goldsmiths Hall to honour the achievements of wounded servicemen and women. And, despite being six months pregnant and entering her third trimester, Meghan continued to travel. She flew to New York to celebrate her baby shower with friends at Café Boulud, and she joined Harry on a short tour of Morocco, draping her pronounced baby bump in a cream Dior dress for a reception held by the British Ambassador in Rabat, and then meeting Crown Prince Moulay Hassan.

In March 2019, Meghan entered her last month of official duties before taking a well-earned rest. She and Harry appeared onstage at Wembley Arena, supporting the WE Day charity event in aid of sustainable international development. On Commonwealth Day, the couple appeared at the Canadian embassy to meet young Canadians living in Britain, and joined the Royal Family at Westminster Abbey for a thanksgiving service. A few days later, the couple commemorated the victims of the mosque attacks in Christchurch by paying a surprise visit to New Zealand House in London. It would be Meghan's last public engagement before she gave birth.

And baby makes three

In their birth announcement, the Sussexes departed from royal protocol in a number of telling ways

The Duke of Sussex could hardly contain his excitement and pride as he stood in front of the television camera on 6 May 2019 outside the stables at Windsor, a stone's throw from his Frogmore Cottage home. The casually dressed prince was obviously overjoyed about the birth of his baby son and he didn't mind who knew it. "As every father and parent will ever say, you know, your baby is absolutely amazing," he gushed, "but this little thing is absolutely to die for, so I'm just over the moon."

The duke shared his immense pride as he joked about getting just two hours' sleep in the night, before calling the birth "the most amazing experience I could ever have possibly imagined". The on-screen interview had not been planned. But clearly Harry was keen to be the one to break the news to the world. Revealing that he was "incredibly proud of his wife", Prince Harry added, "Mother and baby are doing incredibly well. It's been amazing so we just wanted to share this with everybody."

"How any woman does what they do is beyond comprehension," he said. "But we're both absolutely thrilled and so grateful to all the love and support from everybody out there."

Asked if they had any names yet, Harry said: "Still thinking about names. The baby is a little bit overdue, so we've had a little bit of time to think about it." He added, "That's the next bit, but for us I think we will be seeing you guys in probably two days' time as planned, as a family, to be able to share it with you guys and so everyone can see the baby."

"I haven't been at many births," Harry joked. "This is definitely my first birth. It was amazing, absolutely incredible and, as I said, I'm so incredibly proud of my wife."

What was supposed to have happened was that the Palace would reveal to the media by email that Meghan had gone into labour. The Palace's communications department did that just after 2pm on Easter Monday – but in fact by then the duke and duchess had already welcomed their son into the world. Forty minutes later another email dropped from Royal Communications with the key details of the baby's sex, weight and the time of delivery, which sent the waiting media in Windsor into a frenzy.

The statement from the Palace read: "Her Royal Highness the Duchess of Sussex was safely delivered of a son at 0526 hrs. The baby weighs 7lbs 3oz. The Duke of Sussex was present for the birth."

The Palace also announced that Meghan and the baby were "both doing well" and that the Queen and Prince Charles and other members of the Royal Family had been informed. Interestingly, a point was made of saying that Harry's late mother Diana, the Princess of Wales's siblings – the Earl Spencer, Lady Sarah McCorquodale and Lady Jane Fellowes (the baby's great uncle and aunts) – had also been informed.

The statement also revealed that the duchess's mother, Doria Ragland, had been at her daughter's side at Frogmore Cottage. But there was no confirmation or clue as to whether the baby boy had been born at home, as Meghan had wanted, or if she had been surreptitiously whisked away to a hospital in the middle of the night. When the birth certificate finally went public on 17 May it was revealed that the baby had indeed been born at the Portland Hospital in Westminster. It was never revealed whether or not the baby was induced but, since he was overdue, intervention of that sort was a possibility.

In keeping with royal tradition, a framed notice of the birth went on display on a ceremonial easel on the forecourt of Buckingham Palace at 4.30pm on the afternoon following the birth. It was brought out of the Privy Purse Door, carried across the forecourt and placed on the easel where it remained on display until 8pm the next day.

The following day the Prince of Wales, while on a visit to Berlin with the Duchess of Cornwall, said: "We couldn't be more delighted at the news and we're looking forward to meeting the baby when we return."

Previous pages: Harry and Meghan introduce their newborn son, May 2019

Right: The London Eye is lit up in celebration of the royal birth

"Mother and baby are doing incredibly well. It's been amazing so we just wanted to share this with everybody"

The new family Sussex

The Duke and Duchess of Cambridge also expressed their pleasure at the news. Father-of-three William said, "We're thrilled, absolutely thrilled and obviously looking forward to seeing them in the next few days when things have quietened down. I'm glad to welcome my brother to the sleep deprivation society that is parenting."

He joked that he had "plenty of advice" for Harry; but then got serious. "No, I wish him all the best and I hope the next few days they can settle down and enjoy having a newborn in their family and all the joys that come with that."

Kate said, "We're looking forward to meeting him and finding out what his name is going to be so it's really exciting... These next few weeks are always a bit daunting the first time round so we wish them all the best."

The baby boy was now the seventh in line to the throne and positioned behind his father in the line of succession. He had bumped his uncle, the Duke of York, into eighth place. He was expected to take the surname Sussex for school or nursery in the same way as William and Kate's children, George, Charlotte and Louis, took the surname Cambridge.

Twitter was chirruping all day on 6 May. At 6.48am the Royal Family – @Royalfamily – tweeted the birth announcement as it appeared on the ceremonial easel, and went on to say: "The Queen, the Duke of Edinburgh, The Prince of Wales, The Duchess of Cornwall, The Duke and Duchess of Cambridge, Lady Jane

Members of the public await news of the birth outside the gates of Buckingham Palace

Below and opposite: A framed notice of the birth is placed on display in the forecourt of Buckingham Palace

Fellowes, Lady Sarah McCorquodale and Earl Spencer have been informed and are delighted with the news."

Political leaders and famous names took to Twitter to send the following good wishes to the couple. Then Prime Minister Theresa May, said: "Congratulations to the Duke and Duchess of Sussex on the arrival of their baby boy. Wishing you all the best at this happy time." The Archbishop of Canterbury Justin Welby, who married the couple in May 2018, announced: "Congratulations to the Duke and Duchess of Sussex on the birth of their baby boy. May God bless the new family with love, health and happiness."

Then Scottish Conservative Party leader Ruth Davidson, on watching Harry's announcement: "He can barely keep the grin off his face! Lovely stuff. Congratulations to the whole family on their new arrival." Former Prime Minister David Cameron: "Heartfelt congratulations to the Duke and Duchess of Sussex on the arrival of their baby boy. Such wonderful and happy news! Sending love and very best wishes." Then Home Secretary Sajid Javid: "Congratulations to the Duke and Duchess of Sussex on the birth of their boy.

Absolutely wonderful news!" He added, "As Home Secretary, contrary to speculation, I didn't attend the birth!" – a lighthearted reference to the outdated tradition whereby the Home Secretary was required to attend royal births.

The Earl Spencer: "Really very lovely news today – many, many, congratulations! (Good to have another Taurean in the family...)". Michelle Obama, former First Lady of the United States: "Congratulations, Meghan and Harry! Barack and I are so thrilled for both of you and can't wait to meet him." In an Instagram post, the Duke of York said: "Congratulations to the Duke and Duchess of Sussex on the safe delivery of your baby boy!"

His choice of Instagram as the platform to send his greeting was appropriate in the light of the couple's apparent reluctance to start a Twitter account of their own. But back in April they opened their official Instagram page, announcing: "Welcome to our official Instagram; we look forward to sharing the work that drives us, the causes we support, important announcements, and the opportunity to shine a light on key issues. We thank you for your support."

The duke and duchess had made it clear as the birth approached that they did not want to know the sex of the baby until the big day arrived; and they remained true to their word. Once the baby arrived the account announced, on a dark blue background bearing their stylish hallmark: "It's a BOY! Their Royal Highnesses the Duke and Duchess of Sussex are overjoyed to announce the birth of their child."

Harry and Meghan had always insisted there would be a short gap between the birth and their son's first public "engagement" to allow themselves precious private time as a family. They are said to have been desperate to avoid a media circus similar to that surrounding the births of the three children of the Duke and Duchess of Cambridge.

As promised, on 8 May, a few days after Harry's jubilant announcement, a beaming Meghan and Prince Harry introduced their son to the world at a photocall in the Great Hall, Windsor Castle. Just before a meeting with the Queen and Duke of Edinburgh, the Duke of Sussex walked into the room holding his baby son wrapped in a shawl, the duchess close by his side.

"It's magic, it's pretty amazing," Meghan said when asked what being a new mother was like. "I have the two best guys in the world so I'm really happy." She then said of Archie, "He has the sweetest temperament, he's really calm," whereupon Harry quipped, "I don't know who he gets that from."

"He's just been the dream, so it's been a special couple of days," Meghan said. Harry added: "Another great grandchild." Later, when they were asked to show more of their son's face to the cameras, Meghan laughed as Harry joked: "He's

Below and opposite: The proud parents present the newest member of the Royal Family in the Great Hall at Windsor Castle

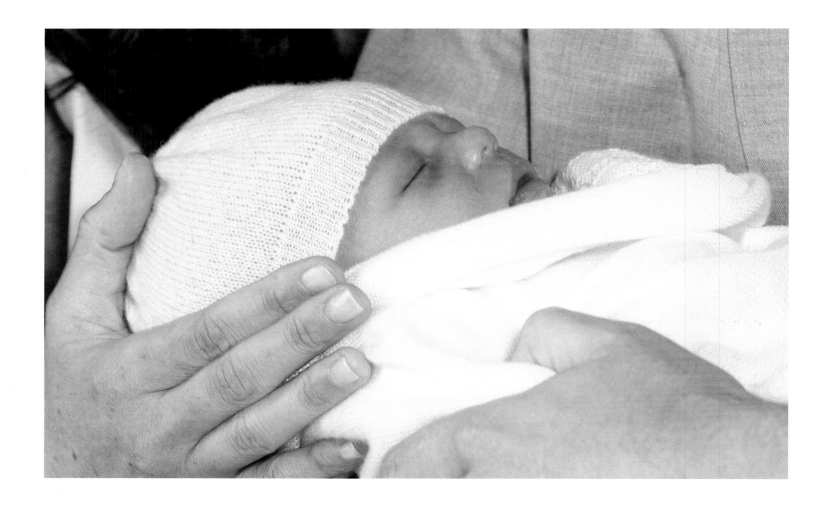

"It's great. We're just so thrilled to have our own little bundle of joy"

already got a little bit of facial hair as well! Wonderful."

"Thank you everybody for all the well wishes and kindness, it just means so much," said Meghan. Harry added, "Everyone says that babies change so much over two weeks; we're basically monitoring how the changing process happens over this next month really. But his looks are changing every single day, so who knows."

Asked how he found parenting, the duke said, "It's great. Parenting is amazing. It's only been two and a half days, but we're just so thrilled to have our own little bundle of joy." Harry said they were looking forward to spending some "precious times with him as he slowly, slowly starts to grow up".

Asked about introducing him to the Queen and the Duke of Edinburgh, Meghan said: "We just bumped into the duke as we were walking by, which was so nice. It'll be a nice moment to introduce the baby to more family; and my mom is with us as well."

The introduction the duchess referred to took place privately at the castle immediately afterwards. Official pictures were released, which showed the baby's maternal grandmother and both the royal great-grandparents gazing adoringly at the new addition to their family. At the Queen's next public engagement that day, an Order of Merit lunch, which she attended with the Duke of Edinburgh, we asked her, "Life is good Your Majesty?" She replied, "Yes, thank you." "Another great-grandchild!" we marvelled, "How many is that now?" to which the Queen proudly replied, "Eight!"

The still images and television footage of Harry and Meghan's photocall, and the ones of them introducing the baby to the Queen and Prince Philip, were beamed across the world and were seen by tens of millions of royal watchers on prime-time breakfast shows in the duchess's own country of birth. A camera crew from the US broadcaster CBS had been added to the select

reporting pool given access to the castle. Its footage was shared among the other US networks.

A child born outside the USA and in wedlock to a US citizen parent and a non-US citizen parent, as in the case of Harry and Meghan, may acquire US citizenship at birth if the US parent has lived in America for five years. The baby therefore had automatic joint citizenship; and American royal enthusiasts followed his progress with even more interest than they did the rest of the Windsors.

Baby Sussex started life in the lap of luxury at the extensively – and expensively – renovated Frogmore Cottage. The builders only finished work on the estate weeks before the birth and it was rumoured that £50,000 had been spent on soundproofing the Windsor property, which is situated on a flight path, to help the baby sleep soundly.

During their engagement, Harry and Meghan lived at Nottingham Cottage in the grounds of Kensington Palace, with William and Kate as neighbours. Harry and Meghan left Kensington Palace and moved to Frogmore Cottage in April 2019, separating their household from that of the Duke and Duchess of Cambridge. It was reported at the time that Harry was keen to "escape the goldfish bowl of royal life for the sake of his marriage and his unborn child".

That determination to escape a life in the public eye brought the couple and their son to Vancouver, Canada and eventually on to Los Angeles in the US, where Meghan was raised and her mother still lives.

Right: The Queen and Prince Harry make their first public appearance following Archie's birth, at St George's Chapel in Windsor Castle

The new family Sussex

A royal introduction

The Sussexes showed their new baby off to the world in the same way as they did everything else: differently

There is perhaps no place on earth that reflects the majesty of monarchy more than St George's Hall, Windsor Castle, the scene of many state banquets. Portraits by Van Dyck, Sir Peter Lely, Sir Godfrey Kneller and Sir Thomas Lawrence hang above the busts of past monarchs and other royal members of the Order of the Garter. Above is a glorious ceiling studded with the coats of arms of every single Knight of the Garter since the order was founded in 1348. The armoured figure on horseback at the east end of the hall is known as "The King's Champion". Traditionally, his role was to ride into the Coronation banquet held in Westminster Hall, throw down his gauntlet three times and challenge anyone to deny the authority of the new sovereign.

For the public introduction of a new baby with no grand title to match his royal lineage, it was perhaps an incongruous setting. But the magnificent and neo-Gothic room designed in the 1820s by Sir Jeffry Wyatville RA, was significant for the baby's parents, the Duke and Duchess of Sussex. The previous year, the first of the two receptions that followed their wedding ceremony had been held there.

Then, it was packed with 600 guests, but on 8 May 2019, the focus was all on just three individuals – Harry, Meghan and their new baby. The royal couple posed with their son for a very select press pool chosen to relay the first pictures of the new family to the waiting world. A veteran royal reporter, Alan Jones of the Press Association, interviewed the couple while his colleague, photographer Dominic Lipinski, shot the stills. Three television cameramen recorded the live footage.

With beatific smiles, the Duke and Duchess of Sussex presented their 7lb 3oz infant to a public impatient to see the first child of dual heritage to be born to a senior member of the Royal Family. The devoted pair seemed beside themselves with joy, giggling and looking lovingly into one another's eyes as they spoke. Harry gently cradled his sleeping son – who was snuggled in a white shawl made from the softest merino wool – in his arms. He was bursting with pride and clearly found it hard to take his eyes off the baby.

"He has the sweetest temperament," confided Meghan, "he's really calm."

"I don't know who he gets that from," joked Harry.

Asked just how it felt to be a dad, Harry replied,

"It's great. Parenting is amazing. It's only been two and a half days... three days, but we're just so thrilled to have our own little bundle of joy."

The duchess went on to describe her feelings on becoming a mother. "It's magic, it's pretty amazing," she cooed. "I have the two best guys in the world so I'm really happy."

Asked who they thought he took after, Megan said, "We're still trying to figure that out." Harry added, "Everyone says that babies change so much over two weeks we're basically monitoring how the changing process happens over this next month really. But his looks are changing every single day, so who knows."

At the request of the press, the couple showed a little more of their son's face to the cameras, which zoomed in on his cute features. "He's already got a little bit of facial hair as well," quipped Harry. "Wonderful!"

"Thank you everybody for all the well-wishes and kindness," said Meghan, as the interview finished. "It just means so much."

The announcement of baby Sussex's name only came after he had met his great-grandparents, which he did immediately after Harry and Meghan's interview. The Queen, Archie's maternal grandmother, Doria Ragland, and his paternal great-grandfather, Prince Philip, beamed with delight as they contemplated the baby, who slept serenely throughout.

"The devoted pair seemed beside themselves with joy, giggling and looking lovingly into one another's eyes as they spoke"

Previous pages and above:
Harry and Meghan introduce
their newborn son in the grand
setting of St George's Hall,
Windsor Castle

Baby Sussex

By deciding to call their son Archie Harrison Mountbatten-Windsor, Harry and Meghan had deliberately chosen not to use a title for him. Perhaps their insistence that there was no need for him to have an aristocratic or royal title was the strongest indication yet that they did not want to raise him in a formal royal way. After all, Archie means "genuine", "bold" or "brave": arguably all attributes any young person needs to live a fulfilled life and succeed in the world, even if their great-grandmother is the Queen. A year later, it would also link to Harry and Meghan's proposed charity, provisionally entitled "Archewell" – meaning sources of action.

The "meet Archie" photo call was a very different introduction from the much more public first glimpses the world got of the Cambridges' babies – and any other Windsor infants before them. Like their father William and their uncle Harry, babies George, Louis and Charlotte had all been presented to the press and public for the first time on the hospital steps as their parents prepared to take them home. Most interestingly of all, they were always in the arms of their mother. Baby Archie, in contrast, was held for the duration by his father. So although the backdrop to Archie's introduction to the press was steeped in tradition, the Sussexes were every inch the modern family.

Left: A clearly besotted Duke and Duchess of Sussex, who described parenthood as "amazing"

The importance of being Archie

With the name they chose for their firstborn, the Sussexes expressed their intention to bring him up as normally as possible

By deciding to call their son Archie Harrison Mountbatten-Windsor, Harry and Meghan clearly chose not to use a title for their firstborn. As the first son of a duke, Archie could have become the Earl of Dumbarton, one of the Duke of Sussex's subsidiary titles; or he could have been Lord Archie Mountbatten-Windsor. But on revealing his name in May 2019, the Palace announced that his parents had "chosen not to give him a courtesy title at this time". Her Majesty The Queen would have approved this decision.

Whatever their attitude to titular protocols, the duke and duchess definitely departed from convention when they called their baby Archie. It was a surprise choice, and not among the bookmakers' favourites of Alexander, Arthur and Albert. Originally a shortened form of Archibald but now often used in its own right, Archie means "genuine", "bold" or "brave".

Master Archie Harrison Mountbatten-Windsor's second name caused particular excitement in one household. Eight-year-old Harrison Degiorgio-Lewis had met Harry twice at The Royal British Legion's Field of Remembrance at Westminster Abbey, which honours our war dead. The Essex schoolboy, whose uncle Lieutenant Aaron Lewis was killed in Afghanistan in December 2008, was convinced he had influenced the Sussexes' decision. "I meet [Prince Harry] quite a lot and we share the same birthday," said Harrison at the time. His father Brett had been less convinced. "Obviously it's lovely of them if they did name their boy after Harrison," he said, "but no, I have not heard anything." Harry and Harrison shared a 15 September birthday and met first in 2016 and again in 2017. Whatever the truth was, some royal watchers on social media had another plausible theory on the middle name: that the new parents chose it because it literally means "Harry's son".

Mountbatten-Windsor was the surname devised in 1960 for male-line descendants of Queen Elizabeth II and Prince Philip without royal styles and titles. It had occasionally been used by those with styles and titles too, when a surname had been required. The three children of the Duke and Duchess of Cambridge all have the name Cambridge on their birth certificates.

Instead, it was announced the new addition to the Royal Family would simply be called Master Archie Mountbatten-Windsor. Unlike William and Kate's sons, he was not a British Prince. Nor did he have the style "His Royal Highness". At the time, it was said that the duke and duchess had decided to keep it simple, "for now."

Previous pages: Harry and Meghan receive a special gift for Archie from the New York Yankees

Above and opposite: Archie's traditional framed announcement and birth certificate

Had Harry and Meghan wanted Master Archie to be titled a Prince from birth like the children of the Duke and Duchess of Cambridge, The Queen would have needed to issue letters patent. She did this for the Duke and Duchess of Cambridge at the end of 2012, when they were expecting George the following July. The monarch declared that William and Kate's children would be called Their Royal Highnesses and take the title Prince and Princess. The document read: "The Queen has been pleased by Letters Patent under the Great Seal of the Realm dated 31 December 2012 to declare that all the children of the eldest son of The Prince of Wales should have and enjoy the style, title and attribute of Royal Highness with the titular dignity of Prince or Princess prefixed to their Christian names or with such other titles of honour."

Thus, the Queen's letters patent revised King George V's 1917 decree that only the Prince of Wales's eldest son was entitled to be styled His Royal Highness and Prince. Also, according to this document, the daughters and younger sons of the Prince of Wales's eldest son were to be styled as children of a duke. These ducal titles would change to royal titles once the Prince of Wales became King. The Queen's decree ensured that if the Duke and Duchess of Cambridge's eldest child had been a daughter, she would be styled a Princess rather than a Lady, as in Princess Charlotte's case.

Nevertheless, at the time, the Palace clarified that this would only be the case until Prince Charles is King, whereupon the child would become a Prince. Originally, the Duke and Duchess of Sussex were also expected to allow their son to take the title "His Royal Highness"

CERTIFIED COPY   **OF AN ENTRY**
Pursuant to the Births and   **Deaths Registration Act 1953**

BBU 479581

BIRTH		Entry No. 51

Registration district   Westminster   Administrative area
Sub-district Westminster   City of Westminster

1. Date and place of birth   **CHILD**
   Sixth May 2019
   Portland Hospital 209 Great Portland Street, Westminster

2. Name and surname   3. Sex
   Archie Harrison MOUNTBATTEN-WINDSOR   Male

4. Name and surname   **FATHER**
   His Royal Highness Henry Charles Albert David Duke of Sussex

5. Place of birth   6. Occupation
   Paddington, Westminster   Prince of the United Kingdom

7. Name and surname   **MOTHER**
   Rachel Meghan Her Royal Highness The Duchess of Sussex

8.(a) Place of birth   8.(b) Occupation
   California, United States of America   Princess of the United Kingdom

9.(a) Maiden surname   9.(b) Surname at marriage if different from maiden surname
   MARKLE

10. Usual address (if different from place of child's birth)
    Frogmore Cottage Windsor Castle SL4 2JG

11. Name and surname (if not the mother or father)   **INFORMANT**   12. Qualification
    _____   Father

13. Usual address
    (if different from
    that in 10 above) _____

14. I certify that the particulars entered above are true to the best of my knowledge and belief   Signature of informant
    Harry

15. Date of registration   16. Signature of registrar
    Seventeenth May 2019
           D.Mevada
           Deputy Registrar

17. Name given
    after registration, _____
    and surname

Certified to be a true copy of an entry in a register in my custody.

_____ { Depy *Superintendent Registrar* / *Registrar*   Date 17ᵗʰ May 2019
Strike out whichever does not apply

System No. 519019841   CAUTION: THERE ARE OFFENCES RELATING TO FALSIFYING OR ALTERING A CERTIFICATE AND USING
OR POSSESSING A FALSE CERTIFICATE. ©CROWN COPYRIGHT

WARNING: A CERTIFICATE IS NOT EVIDENCE OF IDENTITY.

when Prince Charles succeeded his mother. Since Archie would then be the monarch's grandson through the male line, it was going to be his title by right. This was established in a decree known as the George V convention, which was issued in 1917 to limit the number of royal titles at a given time.

But, as a source said after Archie's name was announced, "It's a case of opt-out, otherwise it's automatic. In the case of the Earl and Countess of Wessex [Prince Edward and his wife Sophie] they elected for their children not to become prince and princesses or take the 'HRH' titles. But when Prince Charles becomes King, all children and grandchildren on the direct male line of the sovereign are automatically HRH."

As it now stands, Master Archie – who is still seventh in line to the throne – will not take the full title of HRH "at the appropriate time" as had originally been expected. It seems the Sussexes have well and truly opted out.

"Whatever their attitude to titular protocols, the duke and duchess definitely departed from convention when they called their baby Archie"

The new family Sussex

Above: Harry shakes hands with Harrison Degiorgio-Lewis at Westminster Abbey in 2016

A private function

Archie's christening showed that the Sussexes were
more determined than ever to do things their way

Anyone not on the guest list who wanted to catch a glimpse of baby Archie Harrison Mountbatten-Windsor on the day of his christening stood to be disappointed. On his parents' insistence, this notable event was going to be a strictly private affair. And that in itself is not unusual. Christenings are among the few milestones the Royal Family continues to ring-fence as private celebrations. But the Sussexes' choice of venue – in the private chapel at Windsor Castle – would shield the event from the public gaze and limit the number of guests present.

There would be no television coverage; and no access would be granted to press photographers or reporters, even to record the arrival of guests at a distance. The only people in attendance would be the Duke and Duchess of Sussex's family and close friends – a maximum of 25 people. To the chagrin of the media, even the customary announcement of the godparents' names would not be forthcoming, apparently according to the wishes of those who had been chosen. It was argued that as they were private individuals, not public figures, they had the right to remain anonymous.

On the Wednesday before the event, the palace announced that Archie's baptism would take place on Saturday 6 July. In those three intervening days and speculation about the occasion reached fever pitch.

Harry and Meghan's request to keep their son's christening off limits – as a number of royal baptisms had been previously – was understandable. But its proximity to the revelation that almost £2.5 million of taxpayers' money had been spent on renovating their family home, Frogmore Cottage, in the grounds of Windsor Castle, led to questions about visibility. It prompted the press to ask whether the costly couple offered value for money, given that Harry was now only sixth in line to the throne. And it seemed the more these matters escalated in the media, the more entrenched the couple became.

The event itself passed off smoothly. Baby Archie was duly christened by the Church of England's most senior priest: the Archbishop of Canterbury, the Most Reverend Justin Welby. Photographs were issued later to the media, taken by personal photographer Chris Allerton, a favourite of the couple, who had also taken their wedding photos. He captured the special moment with two pictures, which were released to the public and posted on the Sussexes' Instagram account. He said he was "honoured" to take the official photographs and to be "part of such a joyous occasion".

Formal christenings are required for royal babies because the Queen is, after all, Defender of the Faith and Supreme Governor of the Church of England. They used to be performed within weeks of the birth but today they tend to take place a few months later. Archie was exactly two months old at his christening, about the same age as Prince Louis and Princess Charlotte had been at theirs.

Prince George had been christened when he was three months old and, as is traditional for the future monarch

Above: The changing of the guards
outside Windsor Castle on the day
of Archie's christening, July 2019

Opposite: The occasion was
presided over by the Archbishop
of Canterbury, Justin Welby

of the House of Windsor, at Buckingham Palace. Princess Charlotte's ceremony was held more openly at St Mary Magdalene Church in Sandringham, while Prince Louis was christened at Chapel Royal, St James's Palace, at the age of 11 weeks.

Archie's father, Prince Harry, was baptised at St George's Chapel, Windsor Castle, on 21 December 1984 when he was three months old. Archie was christened in the same royal christening gown, as were his cousins (all three of the Cambridge children and Zara and Mike Tindall's daughters Mia and Lena). The garment – a replica of the intricate lace and satin gown made for Queen Victoria's eldest daughter – has been used for royal infants for the past 11 years.

The new gown was created by the Queen's dresser and personal assistant Angela Kelly and the team of dressmakers at Buckingham Palace, and features the same lengthy skirt, elaborate collars and bow as its predecessor. The original robe was made in 1841 by Janet Sutherland, the daughter of a coal miner from Falkirk, and it entered the record books after being used by 62 royal babies during its lifespan. Styled after the wedding dress Queen Victoria had worn for her marriage to Prince Albert in 1840, the gown was made of Spitalfields silk with a Honiton lace overlay. For 163 years, it was worn by all royal babies, including the Queen, Prince Charles and Archie's uncle Prince William. It was washed in spring water after each ceremony before being stored in a dark room. But by 2004, this precious antique garment had become too fragile to use, so the Queen commissioned a handmade copy.

Traditionally, newlyweds would keep the top tier of their wedding cake for the christening of their first child, just like William and Kate did with their seven-tier fruit cake. Fruit cakes, which for years were the traditional wedding cake of choice, can be stored for years, but sponge cakes should generally be eaten within two to three days. That ruled out Harry and Meghan's layered lemon and elderflower sponge wedding cake, which represented a radical departure from tradition and was not constructed in tiers.

As a rule, royal babies usually have more than the standard three godparents, known as sponsors. Prince George has seven, Princess Charlotte has five and the

youngest of the trio, Prince Louis, has six. There was a lot of speculation as to who was asked to sponsor Archie. Meghan's best friend, the Canadian stylist Jessica Mulroney, was widely tipped. Another of her friends, the tennis legend Serena Williams, ruled herself out. She was busy playing tennis at Wimbledon on the Saturday of the baptism.

It later emerged that among those chosen to sponsor Archie included Tiggy Pettifer (formerly Tiggy Legge-Bourke), wife of former Coldstream Guards officer, Charles Pettifer. As Harry and William's former nanny, she looked after the princes between 1993 and 1999 at their father's behest and became like a mother figure to them in the aftermath of the death of Diana, Princess of Wales. Harry and William are godfathers to her sons Fred and Tom.

One of Archie's male sponsors was later revealed to be Mark Dyer, the princes' mentor and friend. The former equerry to the Prince of Wales, "Marko" became a key figure in both William and Harry's formative years.

The former Welsh Guards officer advised them on their military careers and remained one of Harry's closest friends. Dyer, who runs several pubs in west London, which Harry visits from time to time, joined Harry's close friend Charlie van Straubenzee as the only other of Archie's godfathers to have been identified. These names were not revealed at the time but later, when Harry and Meghan were planning their new life.

The guest list of 25 attendees remained private, too. The Duke and Duchess of Cambridge attended but were not thought to have brought their children with them. Archie's grandfather, the Prince of Wales, and the Duchess of Cornwall reportedly arrived at the ceremony by helicopter and Meghan's mother, Doria Ragland, was also there. The Queen, who had been present at the christenings of most of her other great-grandchildren, did not attend, owing to a prior engagement.

"The Duke and Duchess of Sussex are overjoyed to share the happiness of this day," said a Royal

Opposite and this page:
Three of Archie's godparents
– Mark Dyer (opposite), Tiggy
Pettifer (right) and Charlie van
Straubenzee (below, centre)

The new family Sussex

Communications spokesman, "and would like to thank everyone around the world for their ongoing support. They feel so fortunate to have enjoyed this special moment with family and Archie's godparents."

Along with dressing their baby in the christening gown, the couple did follow other royal traditions. The ornate Lily Font, commissioned by Queen Victoria and Prince Albert for the baptism of their first child Victoria, Princess Royal, in 1841, was also used, as was water from the River Jordan for the actual baptism. The Lily Font is part of the Royal Collection and is now kept at the Tower of London's Jewel House when not in use. It is decorated with lilies and ivy foliage around the rim, features three cherubs around the base, and the main bowl is a large lily bloom. Members of the St George's Chapel Choir performed at the ceremony.

Chris Allerton's photographs of the occasion contained some traditional elements but also a few departures from the protocol of previous Windsor baptisms. One of these photos was a family group shot featuring Archie, Meghan, Harry, Prince William, Kate, the Prince of Wales, Camilla, and Lady Sarah McCorquodale and Lady Jane Fellowes, the sisters of the late Princess of Wales. The second photo was a touching shot of the family of three, with Meghan holding Archie and Harry standing close with his hand on Meghan's arm.

In the larger family photo, Kate wore Princess Diana's Collingwood pearl earrings, the same ones that Diana wore to Harry's christening in 1984. In the photo, Harry and Meghan can be seen sitting on a gold bench with green brocade pattern, the same

Above and opposite: Princess Elizabeth, the future Queen, and Prince Charles both wore the christening gown that was made for Queen Victoria's eldest daughter in 1841

The new family Sussex

Above: Prince Harry, pictured
with his mother on the day of
his christening, December 1984

Opposite: Prince George with his
parents William and Kate at his
christening, October 2013

seat that Princess Diana and the Queen sat on for the official photographs from Harry's christening. In the original photo from 1984, Harry lay in Diana's arms and a two-year-old Prince William sat with his grandmother the Queen.

The couple also broke with tradition by not revealing the exact time of the christening. However, in the group photo the clock on the mantelpiece – a Benjamin Lewis Vulliamy dating back to the early 19th century – showed the time as 11.55am. It suggests that Archie was christened at around 11am.

The decision to include Diana's sisters in the main family group photograph was a powerful statement as they were not featured in the christening photos for Prince George, Princess Charlotte and Prince Louis. But both Lady Jane Fellowes and Lady Sarah McCorquodale have remained close to Harry. Lady Jane was among the first people to visit Harry and Meghan following the birth of Archie on 6 May 2019. She met her

nephew's son even before his brother and sister-in-law, the Duke and Duchess of Cambridge, did.

Harry's aunts, along with his maternal uncle, were also named in Archie's initial birth announcement from Buckingham Palace. It read: "The Queen, The Duke of Edinburgh, The Prince of Wales, The Duchess of Cornwall, The Duke and Duchess of Cambridge, Lady Jane Fellowes, Lady Sarah McCorquodale and Earl Spencer have been informed and are delighted with the news."

After the christening, unhappy royal commentators continued to argue that, as senior Windsors who were funded by the Sovereign Grant, Harry and Meghan were guilty of "having it both ways". Ingrid Seward, editor-in-chief of *Majesty* magazine, who has written about royal children for several decades, said she could not remember an occasion when the names of godparents of a Windsor of Archie's status were ever withheld. "The trouble is that [Harry and Meghan] want it every which way they can," she said.

Despite the media furore, most members of the public were largely sympathetic about Harry and Meghan's stated desire to bring Archie up out of the public spotlight as much as possible. "Meghan and Harry want this to be a completely private moment, very much in keeping with how they've said they wanted to raise this baby," said *Vanity Fair* correspondent Katie Nicholl.

It may have been a major contributor to the Sussexes' decision to step back – and ultimately step down – from their roles as senior members of the Royal Family. But Harry and Meghan showed, from the outset, that they were determined to retain their family privacy, particularly in these early months of Archie's life.

"Harry and Meghan's request to keep their son's christening off limits – as a number of royal baptisms had been previously – was understandable"

Above: A young Prince William entertains those gathered on the day of his brother's christening

The new family Sussex

Father ahead

Despite Harry's desire to do his parenting away from the spotlight, it's not hard to predict the kind of dad he will be

When Harry turned 30 in 2014, the media quizzed him about his intentions of settling down and starting a family. The prince blushed but was typically candid. He said he was waiting for the right moment – and the right woman – to come along.

In May 2015, during a hugely successful solo tour of New Zealand, Harry told Sky News: "Of course, I would love to have kids right now, but there's a process that one has to go through." He summed up his romantic experiences and expectations philosophically. "There come times when you think now is the time to settle down, or now is not, whatever way it is, but I don't think you can force these things; it will happen when it's going to happen."

Harry was single then. But little did he know that within a matter of months his world was to change forever. On a blind date in 2016 with a glamorous American actress, Meghan Markle, "all the stars were aligned", as he later said, and he realised he had met his Miss Right. "Everything was just perfect."

Within weeks he persuaded her to join him in Botswana, South Africa where they camped out under the stars and got to know each other better in a setting where they could really by themselves. It was the start of the celebrated royal romance that would result in a fairy-tale wedding at St George's Chapel, Windsor on 19 May 2018.

A year later, the one time "royal rebel" was ready to embrace fatherhood with gusto as not only a hands-on dad but also a loving and supporting husband. He looked blissfully happy, fulfilled and at peace with himself, his past torments behind him.

Ennobled by his grandmother the Queen, the Duke of Sussex had transformed into a role model that many young people look up to. As a roving Commonwealth ambassador, he earned the Queen's respect by carrying out several royal tours abroad.

Then with Meghan – a dual-heritage woman with a wealth of life experience – by his side, he forced the institution of royalty to move with the times. He and Meghan seemed to be going even further than William and Kate in paving the way for a new kind of royal family, one where dad does even more than changing nappies, helping to cook and doing the school run.

Harry's childhood was not one he would have wished on his own child. He was thrust into the spotlight from the minute his late mother Princess Diana and father Prince Charles first introduced him to the world on 15 September 1984. With his elder brother William by his side, Harry was set for a vastly different upbringing than that of any other child, even though Diana strove hard to give them the most normal upbringing she could. She may have taken them to fast food restaurants and theme parks, but both brothers always knew they were different.

Tragically, fate robbed him of his mother at the age of 12 when Diana died in the Paris car crash that was to change the monarchy forever. Most people remember the poignant sight of Harry on the long public procession behind his mother's coffin, which carried a wreath and card addressed to "Mummy" in an agonised childish script. Harry later recalled the inhumanity of that act of duty, pointing out that he would not have been put through such an ordeal

Previous pages: The Duke of
Sussex meets a young local
during his tour of South Africa
in September 2019

Above: Charles, Harry and
William look at floral tributes to
Diana, Princess of Wales outside
Kensington Palace, 1997

Opposite: Prince Harry visits the
children's ward at The Queen
Elizabeth II Hospital in Bridgetown,
Barbados, 2010

today. He explained that the loss of his mother had instilled feelings deep inside him that he would later be forced to confront for the sake of his sanity.

At 16, Eton-educated Harry confessed to his father to having smoked marijuana on numerous occasions, prompting Charles to send his son to a rehab clinic for the day. But this did not put a stop his drinking and partying and he was photographed, his face flushed, leaving nightclubs after altercations with the paparazzi.

At the age of 20 the "hell-raising" prince found himself in trouble again, this time for wearing a Nazi uniform to a private fancy dress party. He later apologised in a statement saying: "[I am] very sorry if I caused any offence or embarrassment to anyone... It was a poor choice of costume and I apologise."

But perhaps the biggest scandal of all came in 2012 when, at the age of 28, Harry appeared naked in photographs taken at a private party in Las Vegas and then published. Feeling ashamed for embarrassing his family but angry at the media for publishing the photos, Harry – who was in the army at the time – released a statement: "At the end of the day I was in a private area and there should have been a certain amount of privacy that one should expect. It was probably a classic example of me being too much army and not enough prince. It's a simple case of that."

Prince Harry, who served in the army for a decade, attained the rank of Captain and undertook two tours of Afghanistan, certainly won the support of his army comrades. After the nude photos scandal more than 14,000 members of the military came out in solidarity with him and posted shots online of themselves naked. "'Prince Harry' was sort of pushed aside by them but also by me," he said of his days in the army. "When you wear that uniform, you're part of that team." The lessons he learned about working with others towards a common goal are ones he will presumably impart to his son.

After the Las Vegas incident, and after what he described as "two years of total chaos", Harry finally sought counselling – with William's encouragement. He realised he needed help to deal with suppressed feelings he had bottled up after Diana's death. Looking back in 2017, Harry said: "My way of dealing with it was sticking my head in the sand, refusing to ever think about my mum, because why would that help? It's only going to make you sad. It's not going to bring her back."

His experience inspired him to help others who had suffered with mental health issues. Both he and William have been informed by their own experiences of emotional distress and recovery and put these to positive use. They have both spoken out about mental health issues and the

Above and opposite: Harry at the official opening of the Sentebale Mamohato Children's Centre in Lesotho, 2015

need to address trauma, particularly in childhood, rather than running away from it or suppressing it. Together with their wives, the princes launched the Heads Together initiative to help people address "everyday" mental health. All four parents are likely to be more switched on to the mental-health needs of their children.

The loss of Diana has also given Harry an unusual degree of compassion and insight into the lives of traumatised children. In a speech at a children's centre in Lesotho in 2015, he said, "The children at the centre were much younger than me [when my mother died] and of course, their situation was a great deal more challenging than my own. Nonetheless, we shared a similar feeling of loss, having a loved one – in my case a parent – snatched away so suddenly."

There is no question that Princess Diana's devotion to numerous deserving causes, together with her more modern, altruistic approach to monarchy, has inspired both her sons. Harry and Meghan have both been encouraged by their parents to respect and help others. "We don't want to be just a bunch of celebrities, but instead use our role for good," he said in 2017. "You've got to give something back. You can't just sit there." There's no doubt they will pass these values on through their parenting.

Princess Diana's unhappy union with Charles has encouraged her boys to enter into love marriages with women whose interests and values complement and support

their own. The two Duchesses can expect their husbands to be supportive, especially when it comes to the business of parenting. And the love between the Sussexes really shows. In all their public appearances, they are demonstrative and loving towards each other, with one always extending a supportive hand to the other, literally showing they have each other's back. As both come from broken homes, it will be important to them to demonstrate to their children that they are in love and united.

Another lesson from Diana's legacy that her sons were keen to apply when rearing their own children was the one relating to excessive media intrusion. Since Harry and Meghan were further down the line of succession they hoped to escape some of the attention the Cambridges and their children attract, especially as they live in Kensington Palace and attend London schools. Even then William and Kate have done much to ensure that the press stand back from their daily life and only photograph the children at official occasions.

The Sussexes said all along that they wanted to go further to protect their children from the prying eyes of the press. At the time they hoped that leaving Nottingham Cottage in Kensington Palace – on the frontline of royal exposure – for the more secluded environs of Frogmore Cottage would help achieve this.

Unfortunately, the move away from the capital did not deter Splash News Agency from sending snooping

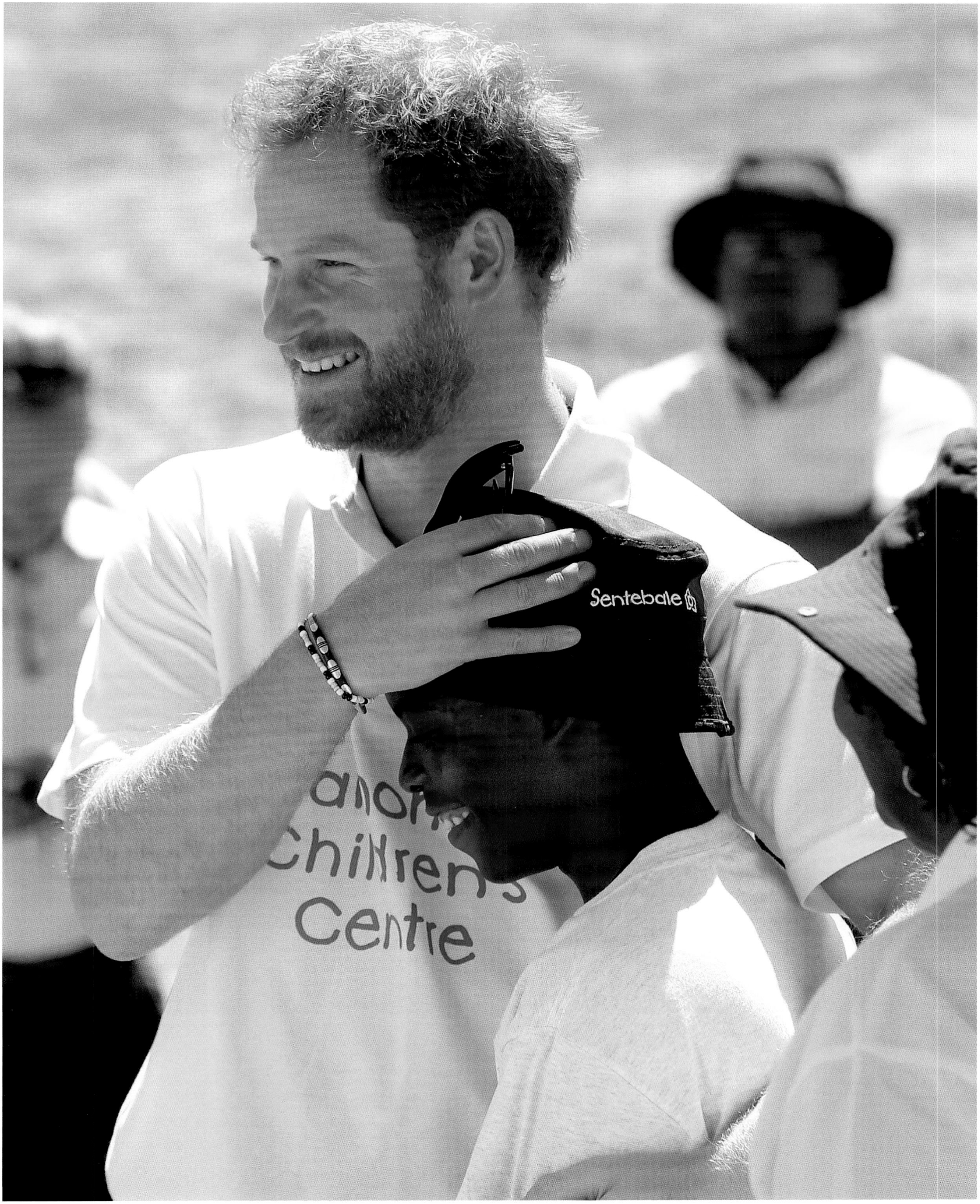
Sentebale
Centre

Above: Harry and Meghan make their way through Windsor following their wedding ceremony, May 2018

paparazzi to fly close to the Sussexes' home in a helicopter and take intrusive pictures of the living room, dining area and even the bedroom. When this incident occurred in January 2019, the security risks it presented meant the duke and duchess were obliged to find alternative temporary accommodation. They took legal action against the publication responsible and only moved back in to Frogmore Cottage in April of that year, in time for Archie's birth. A month later Harry was awarded substantial damages for the intrusion, which were donated to charity after legal costs had been covered. The agency apologised and promised not to repeat the exercise.

Harry is clearly a protective father but also, if his attitude to his nephews and niece is anything to go by, a fun one. When George was born in 2013 and made him an uncle, Harry vowed that his mission was to "make sure he has a good upbringing, to keep him out of harm's way and to make sure he has fun." We can safely assume that Archie is bound to be getting all that and more from his father.

The former First Lady, Michelle Obama, confirmed that he had achieved at least part of this ambition when she appeared with Harry in a sofa chat on *Good Morning America* in 2017. She was asked about a visit she had made to Kensington Palace the previous year, at which both George and Harry were present. She described how Harry must have been on his best behaviour because a baffled George kept asking him, "Uncle Harry, why are you so quiet?" Harry conceded that it was indeed because "usually I'm throwing him around the room and stuff".

"Harry's childhood was one he would not have wished on his own child"

Michelle Obama meets Prince Harry at Kensington Palace during the global tour of her Let Girls Learn initiative, June 2015

Anyone can see that his delight in the company of children is genuine. "I get a huge buzz spending time with kids," he has said. And another thing he learned from his mother, which contributes to his fun side, is that it's okay to be naughty, "as long as you don't get caught."

Harry's love for his mother is well known. Less often talked about but just as important – if not more so, given his role as a father – is his excellent relationship with Prince Charles. Their bond seems to have grown, if anything, even stronger since Charles demonstrated his approval of Meghan by walking her up the aisle at the Sussexes' wedding. Harry's account of his father's support in more difficult times, when Princess Diana died, is equally revealing. Harry told the BBC in 2017, "He was there for us, he was the one out of two left, and he tried to do his best and make sure we were protected and looked after."

In keeping with the Sussexes' more progressive style, and perhaps echoing the ecological concerns of his father, Harry has voiced his concerns about the future of the planet in relation to responsible parenthood. At a roundtable discussion with young leaders from the Queen's Commonwealth Trust (QCT) in 2019, Harry said, "As someone who is about to become a father, I am acutely aware of our shared responsibility to make this world more resilient and its inhabitants more accountable for the next generation."

Opposite: Harry is presented with a bespoke babygrow at the launch event for the Invictus Games 2020 in May 2019

Below: A girl gives the prince a gift at the same event, May 2019

The new family Sussex

The Duke of Sussex makes a friend during walkabout in Auckland, New Zealand, October 2018

In March 2020, as Harry and Meghan wound up their royal duties as senior members of the Royal Family, they invited the QCT young leaders to a roundtable at Buckingham Palace, an event they posted on their Instagram page. Topics under discussion included mental health, equal opportunities and youth leadership in driving positive change to address global challenges. Harry will be leaving his role as Commonwealth Youth Ambassador; but he and Meghan are to remain president and vice-president of the QCT. Their ongoing involvement in the organisation will doubtless continue to inform their parenting.

Harry has described himself as a feminist; and it is no wonder, given the inspiring women he has had in his life, from his great-grandmother the Queen Mother, his grandmother Queen Elizabeth II, through Princess Diana and now Meghan. "Real men treat women with the dignity and respect they deserve," he has said. This will be a great example to his son – and, perhaps, to any future Sussex daughters who might come along.

"We don't want to be just a bunch of celebrities, but instead use our role for good"

Right: Harry receives an impromptu hug from a young fan in Australia, October 2018

The new family Sussex

The chic of it

The Duchess of Sussex has added her own very personal statements to the Windsors' sartorial record

The newly engaged couple stood beaming for the cameras, arms intertwined, Meghan's hand carefully positioned to show off the diamond ring that Prince Harry had crowned her finger with. Meghan was dressed in a minimalist white coat by the Canadian brand Line the Label. She paired it with a green dress and nude Aquazzura heels. The outfit, worn for the couple's engagement photocall in November 2017, was immaculate.

But it was what Meghan wasn't wearing that gave the public its first inkling into the type of style icon she was to become. In the grounds of Kensington Palace she stood, legs bare – not a flesh-coloured pair of nylons in sight. What might have seemed like a minor detail marked Meghan Markle out as a thoroughly modern Windsor bride-to-be and one who wouldn't always play by the establishment's rules.

The wardrobe choices in the House of Windsor are never thrown together hurriedly. Stylists work with family members to select looks and follow strict protocol. The rules that each a member plays by are subtle yet set in place to ensure they strike just the right tone of decency and decorum.

Hats are not to be worn after six o'clock in the evening. Hemlines must be carefully considered and anything daringly floaty is lined with weights. There's even etiquette for the painting of nails: polish must always be nude. As for tights, well, they're part of the Windsor uniform. And each member of the royal family must travel with a black outfit in case a member of the monarchy dies. (This decree was regrettably overlooked when the Queen was touring Africa in 1952 and had to fly home on receiving the news of her father's death. An appropriately sombre dress had to be delivered to her on the landed plane before she could disembark and face the waiting press.) For royals, then, getting dressed in the morning entails so much more than simply picking a favourite skirt; there's an intention behind each look and a careful image that's being cultivated.

With that very first public appearance on the announcement of her engagement, Meghan had begun to write her own sartorial rule book. She had decided her USP was to be the contemporary consort who liked a double-breasted blazer dress and a messy chignon: a look that spoke of the glamorous Hollywood life she once belonged to.

On Meghan's first official evening engagement she gave a further indication that she was determined to modernise the monarchy's fashion credentials. At an awards ceremony – a typically British affair where every outfit was accessorised with an umbrella – Meghan sported a skinny Alexander McQueen trouser suit. It was a far cry from the diplomatic formality favoured by her soon-to-be family.

Each ensemble Meghan has worn since being married to Harry has been documented by an ever-watchful press and an approving public, keen to snap up any items available in the shops. For those designers and high-street labels that Meghan chooses to wear, it's been better for sales than a month of Black Fridays.

When she was spotted at the Invictus Games in Toronto accessorising a crisp shirt with a pair of Finlay & Co. shades, she sparked a 1,000 per cent increase in sales of the sunglasses. And when the black sweater she wore with Burberry wide-legged pants was discovered to be from Marks & Spencer, a stampede among shoppers ensued. Such is the power of the Duchess of Sussex, or the "Meghan Effect".

Of course, Meghan isn't the only fresh face in the Windsor fashion stakes. Catherine, the Duchess of Cambridge, has inspired her own "Kate Effect". Where Meghan favoured minimalism and modernity, Kate's great triumph is in playing the princess, and her effect on the British fashion industry has been colossal.

"There is no question that Kate choosing to wear Reiss has impacted our brand," David Reiss, the high-street label's founder, told *Marie Claire* after the duchess was photographed in one of the brand's dresses. "The surge in web traffic following the release of these images caused our website to crash. The dress promptly sold out online when service was resumed." Similarly, the London designer Matthew Williamson reported that a white chiffon dress that Kate once wore, "sold out straight away. We just couldn't make enough, we sold out of everything we had!" Kate also isn't afraid to recycle her past triumphs – a nod to her middle-class roots, perhaps, that has helped establish her as one of the people. Albeit one of the people with exceptional style.

Her sister-in-law's bolstering of the British fashion industry is something Meghan has emulated in her own way. She was the unofficial guest of honour at the 2018 Fashion Awards, and presented Givenchy's Clare Waight Keller – who designed her wedding dress – with the award for British Designer of the Year Womenswear.

Previous pages: Meghan makes a statement of her own at the announcement of her and Harry's engagement, November 2017

Left: The Duchess of Cambridge has also firmly established her fashion credentials

Opposite: The "Meghan Effect" has resulted in sales of some items increasing tenfold

Above: An elegant Duchess of
Sussex sets off for the evening
reception on her wedding day,
May 2018

Making the right sartorial impression is something Meghan is clearly well versed in. The moment the Duke and Duchess of Sussex announced they were expecting their first child, all eyes were on her and her maternity wardrobe. She upheld her sleek, tailored and minimalist sense of style; and there was not a paisley smock in sight. Instead, at Princess Eugenie's wedding she opted for a perfectly cut navy coat. In Australia, she wore an Oscar de la Renta tulle gown embellished with birds. In Tonga, the duchess wore a scarlet, pleated Self-Portrait dress – a niche choice that had fashion editors applauding. For her first visit to the National Theatre she chose a peach, tailored blazer with matching minidress by designer Brandon Maxwell. Her clothes, even in pregnancy, were undeniably chic.

But Meghan made her biggest fashion statement since her wedding dress when she guest-edited the September issue of British *Vogue* in 2019, in collaboration with the magazine's ultra-cool editor-in-chief, Edward Enninful. Entitled 'Forces for change', it featured 15 women including representing the arts, sport and politics who were making a big impression. In an introduction to the issue Meghan wrote that the idea behind her guest editorship was "to take the year's most-read fashion issue and steer its focus towards the values, causes and people making impact in the world today."

"Through this lens," she said, "I hope you'll feel the strength of the collective in the diverse selection of women chosen for the cover as well as the team of support I called upon within the issue to help bring this to light. I hope readers feel as inspired as I do, by the 'Forces for Change' they'll find within these pages."

This was by no means the first House of Windsor/*Vogue* crossover. *Vogue* readers are no different from other members of the public in regarding certain females in the House of Windsor as style icons they look to for inspiration or just to ogle at their regal otherness. Princess Anne has appeared on the cover three times, while Princess Diana –

"It was what Meghan wasn't wearing that gave the public its first inkling into the type of style icon she was to become"

Meghan made the headlines at the 2018 Fashion Awards

perhaps still the greatest royal fashion influencer of all – clocked up an impressive four covers for the magazine. And *Vogue* chose Kate, the Duchess of Cambridge, to front its 100th anniversary issue, with a 10-page picture spread inside.

But Meghan went one better than being a cover girl on 'The Fashion Bible'. In her capacity as guest editor she got to decide what went on the cover. And although she wasn't the first duchess to collaborate with a media organisation – Kate Middleton had sat in the editor's desk for a day at the *Huffington Post* to highlight children's mental health – this seemed a more daring move, emphasising Meghan's apparent desire to be regarded as relevant as well as fashionable. If anything, this doubled the force of Meghan Effect. The September issue flew off the newsstands faster than any other edition in the history of British *Vogue*.

Like their late mother-in-law before them, both Meghan and Kate are savvy about what their clothes say about them and the roles they must play, aware of how clothes shape their public image. Be it Kate's down-to-earth by day, princess by night appeal or Meghan's sleek elegance and gentle rule-breaking, theirs are styles that refuse to flirt with the whims of fashion. Instead, they have firmly established their places as style icons for our modern age.

Above and opposite: Meghan has torn up the royal rulebook and created her own style

The new family Sussex

Grown-up food for babies

Woodland Wonders creates high-quality organic meals that are a sensory experience for babies – and a guilt-free pleasure for parents

You are what you eat – or so the saying goes. But it's a phrase that doesn't go far enough for Danish entrepreneur Christina Hansen. 'What about *how* you eat?' she says. "The ingredients we put in our bodies are crucial, but the *way* we eat is important too – everything from flavour to texture and environment. It's why adults choose restaurants with great lighting, service and ambiance as well as fantastic food. Why don't we seek to create that rounded experience for babies too?"

This question is at the core of her organic baby food business. With a background in corporate law, Christina sought a career change when she became a mother. In 2009, she stumbled upon an opportunity to work with a UK-based baby development company called Baby Sensory, running classes to stimulate babies' mental and physical development, and eventually gaining the master franchise rights for the Nordic and Benelux regions.

"What I noticed was that, when parents finished the classes, they would grab a jar and start feeding their baby," says Christina. "They'd say it was hard to find high-quality prepared food, and that they didn't have the time or energy to cook from scratch. I decided to start a blog with recipes."

That blog developed into a local business, selling fresh baby meals and cereals. "I produced all the food at home from my basement," she says, "and it really took off." Babies love the flavours, the textures and, yes, the experience. Parents love the guilt-free convenience of giving their children 100 per cent organic, nutritious food that is portable and easy to prepare.

The cereals, branded as Woodland Wonders, were soon picked up by the Danish retail giant Coop and stocked in Copenhagen stores. "The thing is, I produced food as a mother would," says Christina. "I didn't know anything about the industry, I just made food that I wanted to eat and I wanted my children to eat. In those early years, I learned a lot by trying hard and falling flat on my nose! But I'm now a savvy businesswoman. I'm now collaborating with people that deliver to the highest standards and work to my specifications."

The brand has expanded too, with two organic snack bars as well as the range of cereals. Woodland Wonders products are made with dried fruits and oats with no added sugar or additives, and they're stocked in more than 700 stores in Denmark as well as select locations in Norway, Hungary, Greece and the UK. The firm are also excited to be launching in the US later this year.

Christina is proud of her strong brand ethos and identity. "We've created a universe of forest animals, illustrated with bright colours," she explains. "My home in Denmark is next to a forest, which is where I get my inspiration." This goes back to the idea of creating a 360-degree experience. "With the packaging as much as the food, I want to stimulate touch, sight, taste, smell. Food has to be enjoyed on all levels – especially for babies. We need to give them those sensory experiences.'

Her own children, Caroline and Thomas, are now 12 and 14. "Of course, they like soda and crisps at the weekend!" Christina laughs, "but they eat healthily. They have good skin, they're active, they're happy. When you start out with pure, honest ingredient, you set kids up for life. Healthy food and quality ingredients are among life's great luxuries. I want everyone to enjoy them.'
www.woodlandwonders.com

Sustainable Swedish style

Newbie's thoughtful approach to childrenswear has earned the Swedish brand a dedicated following

With a range of beautiful and loveable fashion pieces, all made of either 100 per cent organic cotton or recycled materials, it's easy to see why the Swedish fashion label Newbie has become a natural choice for royalty. Newbie clothes have been seen on pictures of the Swedish royal family, a source of great pride for this label.

Newbie's simple, stylish designs offer a nature-inspired colour palette that varies over the course of the year. "Colours are coordinated from season to season," says Camilla Wernlund, Newbie's International Expansion Manager. "This means that new purchases can be easily combined with existing pieces in your child's wardrobe. This is also what sustainability is about for us."

Its patterns are based on fairy tales, paintings and old wallpaper prints, and are hand-drawn by the team of designers in Gothenburg. "That's something unique in the industry today," says Wernlund. British *Vogue* recently described Newbie as one of "the best sustainable fashion labels for children".

This commitment to an ethical, sustainable approach is stitched into the very fabric of the brand. "We do our utmost to choose sustainable solutions in every aspect of the production process, from how the cotton is grown to working conditions in which they are produced," says Wernlund. "We also want our garments to be passed down from one generation to the next. There is a sizeable second-hand market for Newbie, which is completely in line with our sustainability focus."

Newbie was launched in 2010 as a brand with a long-lasting, sustainable, value-for-money fashion line for babies and kids. The clothes quickly gained a cult following on social media, with fans using the hashtag #Newbielovers and setting up dedicated Facebook groups for buying and selling used Newbie clothes. Thanks to its social-media success, the first stand-alone store opened in Stockholm in 2014. The Newbie brand is now expanded internationally, where its collaborative approach to fashion is game-changing.

"Our customers have contributed to shaping the brand right from the beginning," says Wernlund. "Their engagement constantly inspires the creative team. When they like a particular colour scheme or pattern, it feeds into what we do next. This interaction is a major part of the brand."

When customers asked for clothes for older children, the age range was extended up to eight years old. Newbie has also recently launched a swimwear collection for mothers, plus bed linen and wallpaper. "We are becoming a total lifestyle brand, rather than just a fashion label," Wernlund continues. "On our blog, we have articles on everything from nutritious food to good sleeping habits. It's all about making a sustainable lifestyle easy for parents."

Newbie now has standalone stores in England, as well as branches in the Nordic nations and Poland. "We have a rapidly growing fanbase in the UK," says Wernlund. "We have already won several awards, including Best New Brand at the 2018 Little London Magazine awards, and three gongs at the 2018 Mumii Family Awards. Newbie appeals to all those who care about a conscious way of living."

www.newbiestore.com

Right: Newbie's ethical childreanswear features nature-inspired colours and design

Below: The Swedish label aims to expand worldwide in the future

Carry on in style

Mamalila creates stylish, functional and sustainable jackets specially designed for parents and babies

"Mamalila really started with my kids," says owner Vicki Marx. Her multi-award-winning babywearing jackets were her solution to protecting her babies out of doors when carrying them in a sling. "Using a sling is comfortable and you build a strong bond with your child, but what do you do in bad weather?"

Vicki Marx's solution, launched in 2005, is an innovative garment that adapts from a regular jacket into a babywearing jacket. An insert, zipped onto the jacket's zip, encases the baby's body, keeping it warm and fully protected from cold, wind and rain. Mamalila also makes inserts to enlarge the jackets during pregnancy, both extending their usefulness and reducing waste. "It's about functionality," she says. "Mamalila allows you to make good use out of a good jacket."

It comes as no surprise that Mamalila has won numerous accolades: a German Innovation Award Gold, German Brand Award Gold and a German Design Award, along with gongs from OutDoor Industry and Kind+Jugend. The success of the jackets, which also come in a winter wool version, derives not just from their adaptability, but from their good looks and high quality. "Women who have just had a baby are in a period of change," says Marx. "Having a jacket that is well designed and doesn't look like a baby jacket helps women to get back to looking and feeling good."

Sustainability is a core consideration at Mamalila, which was certified carbon neutral in 2019. Its products, which include jackets for men, are made using carefully sourced organic cotton, recycled polyester and boiled wool. Marx has also created a company that offers flexible employment for women like herself. "I had two kids and I started a company – I didn't want to leave either," she says. "Mamalila is an organisation where the kids always come first and our part-time working mothers can work from home if they need to. It has resulted in a strong, dynamic and devoted team."

Mamalila's attractive and adaptable jackets make it possible for parents to enjoy an active, outdoor lifestyle, keeping their babies close, warm and safe. In setting up the company, Vicki Marx has created a similarly warm and safe working environment. "We make the best babywearing jackets on the market and we all work hard to keep it that way."

www.mamalila.de

Fabric of life

Engel's eco-friendly clothing for
babies and adults are as comfortable
and stylish as they are sustainable

Using fabrics like merino wool, silk
and cotton, Engel products carry
eco-friendly accreditation

Engel makes high-quality baby clothes that are as pure and good for infant skin as they are for the environment. Using certified organic merino virgin wool, silk and cotton, the family-run German company has extended its range to include underwear and clothing up to adult sizes. From its bestselling wool and silk baby bodies to cosy wool terry jackets, Engel has built its reputation on wearable well-being.

Long before sustainability became the clothing industry watchword, Engel was considering every stage of its manufacturing process. "The original company was founded in the 1930s making underwear for babies," explains Managing Director Vera Simon. "In 1982, when my grandparents took it on, they focused on natural textiles produced in Germany without chemicals."

So began the firm's evolution into the environmentally conscious business of today; one which, while upholding ethical employment standards for its 50 or so staff, produces warm, colour-fast clothing using natural, sustainable fibres. Its soft, strong and breathable fabrics are used for baby clothes and adult athletic wear alike.

Most Engel products carry Global Organic Textile Standard (GOTS) certification or Naturtextil IVN Certified Best accreditation – standards for eco-friendly textiles with strict ecological and social requirements. The company has never used harmful azo dyes and only uses renewable materials at its solar and hydraulic-powered factory. "We make superior products that have received standout certifications," says Simon. "We have some other companies that we work with, who make our fabric and sew it, but they are only an hour away. We are not all flying around, so we avoid pollution."

Looking ahead, Engel intends to introduce a scheme to recycle old clothes for new. "We want to produce clothing using recycled fibres to reduce waste," says Simon.

For consumers who want the reassurance of a quality product that is manufactured without harming the planet, Engel offers the highest levels of environmental and social sustainability. As for its smallest customers, it would seem its softly coloured and comfortable clothing is as big a hit with them as with their parents.
www.engel-natur.de

Chapter two

A YEAR TO REMEMBER

Archie's debut engagement

During the Sussexes' South African tour, the world was waiting to witness Archie's first public appearance. It was not disappointed

"Arch meets Archie," ran Harry and Meghan's official Instagram account, accompanied by a video of a gurgling boy, smiling and laughing for the cameras. Here was little Archie, just four-and-a-half months old, sat on his mother's knee opposite one of the towering figures of the 20th century – the Most Reverend Archbishop Desmond Tutu. As debut official engagements go, the meeting was a huge success – a heartwarming blend of youth and experience.

It was also somewhat in contrast to some of the more uneasy moments of the Sussexes' September 2019 tour of South Africa – a tour that proved an emotional awakening for the prince, now a father and husband. The official visit to the place he had gone to try to process the loss of his mother, Diana, Princess of Wales, seemed to stir up unresolved, dormant issues from the time of her passing. On every occasion when he spoke publicly he mentioned her. His memories of loss were vivid, his pain raw.

Rightly or wrongly, Harry aired his inner feelings in an emotional outburst about media intrusion in an ITV film fronted by his long-standing friend, broadcaster Tom Bradby. Harry also unleashed his pent-up anger towards the tabloid press in a statement he wrote himself on the couple's official website. It came at the same time that Meghan started legal action against the *Mail On Sunday* over a claim that it had unlawfully published a private letter to her father, Thomas Markle.

To many, Harry's behaviour seemed a little out of place. After all, it had been a hugely successful official visit and the media coverage throughout had been very positive. The couple had been lauded in the press for their visit to Nyanga township in the Cape Flats just outside of Cape Town. Perhaps some of the media coverage Meghan received once the euphoria of the wedding had died down was a little snippy, but nothing more. Was the couple, wrapped in their newborn baby bubble, guilty of oversensitivity? Whatever the truth was, Meghan was clearly finding being part of the Royal Family difficult and this was her cry for help.

She complained that she had been left to fend for herself. She was brought close to tears as she described on camera her struggles with constant press scrutiny, especially as a new mother. When ITV's Tom Bradby asked her how she was coping, Meghan's eyes welled up as she answered, "Not many people have asked if I'm okay".

"Look," she said, "any woman – especially when they are pregnant – you're really vulnerable and so that was made really challenging, and then when you have a newborn – you know? And especially as a woman, it's a lot. So you add this [media attention] on top of just trying to be a new mom or trying to be a newlywed it's, well…" Ironically, this somewhat shaky and emotional appearance was filmed in a setting that had provided the backdrop for some of the most delightful and upbeat royal photographs ever taken on a royal tour.

The accredited press present on the trip had been promised there would be a photo opportunity involving baby Archie; but the couple and their aides remained tight-lipped as to when and where this would actually take place.

As it transpired, the occasion was held at Archbishop Desmond Tutu's Legacy Foundation in Cape Town in the presence of the great man – a Nobel Peace Prize winner and champion of the anti-apartheid movement. The handful of press representatives invited had not been told that Archie would make an appearance but, given the prominence of the host and the relatively private setting – Harry, Meghan and Archie had been invited to tea – there was a good chance it might happen. Their speculation proved to be correct. As the select few were ushered into the open courtyard, Sara Latham, Harry and Meghan's media director, revealed that this was to be the moment when Archie made his international debut.

The unveiling of Archie on day three of the 10-day Africa tour was inspired. He had missed all the previous engagements, being looked after by his nanny while Harry and Meghan went about their official business. But in this intimate setting, Archie was finally brought before the cameras. In cute blue-and-white-striped dungarees, the baby smiled and laughed like a natural performer as the couple took tea with the Archbishop.

*Previous pages, opposite and
above: Harry, Meghan and Archie
arrive at Archbishop Tutu's Legacy
Foundation in Cape Town*

A year to remember

Above: The meeting between the Sussexes and Archbishop Tutu was a heartwarming affair

Also present were his wife, Nomalizo Leah Tutu, and daughter, Thandeka Tutu-Gxashe, who runs a campaign that provides portable desks for schoolchildren. She suggested the baby must have cameras in his genes, what with a much-photographed prince for a father and an actress for a mother. "I think he's used to it already," said Harry as the cameras recorded the historic moment for the rest of the world. Meghan was more pensive. "He's an old soul," she said.

Warm and smiling throughout the visit, Archbishop Tutu, 87, was full of praise for Harry and Meghan. "Thank you for your concern and interest in the welfare of our people," he said. "It's very heartwarming to realise that you really, genuinely are caring people. We all try to make things better." Prince Harry was handed two photographs, one for him and one for his brother William, showing their mother pictured with Nelson Mandela in Cape Town in 1997.

Tutu, who campaigned tirelessly for Mandela's release, set up the legacy foundation with his wife to help instil their values in the next generation of leaders. Its chair, Niclas Kjellström-Matseke, said: "We are enormously grateful to welcome the duke and duchess to our magnificent space, and for their love and respect for 'the Arch'."

The Legacy Foundation was a fitting setting for the first filmed appearance of the first Windsor baby of dual heritage. It is housed in an old Cape Dutch granary that was built by slaves, where it carries on the

"Little Archie sat on his mother's knee opposite one of the towering figures of the 20th century"

work done by the Archbishop, who chaired the Truth and Reconciliation Commission. This body was a court-like, restorative justice body assembled after the end of apartheid. It played a large part in South Africa's peaceful transition from whites-only rule to full and free democracy and Nelson Mandela's presidency.

In the video posted by Harry and Meghan after the occasion, Meghan is featured carrying Archie and making soothing sounds. He is laughing and gurgling as the trio walk through a courtyard towards some stairs, where Archbishop Tutu emits a cry of joy as he greets them. He is then photographed kissing the baby on the forehead. The photographic record is historic, the 30-minute meeting one to remember. Tutu, who was prominent in the liberation struggle during Nelson Mandela's long imprisonment, said he was "thrilled" by the "rare privilege and honour" of meeting the couple and little Archie.

Opposite and below: Archie wore
a pair of striped dungarees for the
memorable meeting

"In cute blue-and-white-striped dungarees, the baby smiled and laughed like a natural performer as the couple took tea with the Archbishop"

At a later engagement, Meghan was guest of honour at a meeting of mothers2mothers, an organisation which employs women living with HIV as community health workers called Mentor Mothers. She sat in a circle and, after hearing what they do to help other mothers, said, "The work that's being done here is really special. I see how having that shared experience creates a much stronger result."

After accepting a gift of a framed photograph of women that mothers2mothers had helped, she told her hosts: "I just thought that, in the spirit of community, what's so nice is to be able to share some of the things that we have at home as well. "And so we can obviously make sure everything you need is provided for you, but we've brought some of the things that my friends and I used for our kids and Archie, that don't fit any more." She had brought with her a large black holdall full of baby clothes to donate to the organisation. "Here's a few little things that I thought would be helpful," she said, producing two vests with lettering on them and holding them up one by one. "The Future," she said. "And he's outgrown his Invictus one."

Gesturing to the bag, she added: "There's all sorts of things there. It's so important to be able to share with other families. You're all in this together and with each other and so we just wanted to share something from our home [with] each of yours."

Now we are one

Archie's first year has been a momentous one, for his doting parents and his royal British relations alike

Meghan could not have looked prouder as she shared a major life update about her son Archie. The duchess, who was visiting Robert Clack Upper School in Dagenham, east London for International Women's Day – one of her last appearances as a senior royal – smiled broadly when she was asked about her precious baby.

The question came from Geraldine Dear, one of the real-life heroines whose 1968 campaign for equal pay for women at the Ford car plant in Essex inspired the film *Made In Dagenham*. She described her exchange with the duchess during her visit to the school. "She said to me, '[Archie's] exactly 10 months today and he's just trying to walk!'" It was clear from Dear's account that although Archie was an ocean and thousands of miles away, Meghan was in daily contact with him – and brimming with maternal pride at his next imminent milestone.

One of the students who got to speak to Meghan that day, 18-year-old Olivia Collins, recounted their conversation. "She was talking about how having Archie has changed her life," Collins said, "and how important motherhood is."

In a separate public appearance, this time at the Endeavour Fund Awards, the duchess told guest Claire Spencer, "He is 10 months now and is into everything." It seemed that everywhere Meghan and Harry went on their final series of royal visits in March this year, Archie was at the forefront of their minds and they didn't mind sharing information about him with the people they met.

It was a pleasant surprise for the reporters following the duchess on these engagements to find her speaking so openly about little Archie. After all, the Sussexes have been intent on safeguarding their baby's privacy since his birth.

Indeed, much to the disappointment of the Royal Family, the couple had decided to leave Archie behind this time, to be cared for by his nanny in Canada while they returned to the UK. The internal clock disruption he would have suffered as a result of two transatlantic flights must have been a major consideration. But another important factor in Harry and Meghan's decision not to bring him was probably their desire to protect him from press attention.

The Queen was said to be sad, understandably, at missing out on what would be her last opportunity for some time to spend precious time with her youngest great-grandchild. She might well feel that Archie growing up abroad and seeing so little of his British great-grandparents, aunts, uncles and cousins is one of the biggest downsides to the Sussexes' relocation overseas.

Privately, the 93-year-old monarch is said to have told Harry in meetings they had at Windsor Castle that she hoped Archie would still spend time with the Royal Family so that he would have the chance to develop a relationship with them and vice versa. This may have influenced her invitation to the Sussexes to spend the summer with her and the rest of the royals at Balmoral, her estate in the Scottish Highlands. At any rate, they are understood to have accepted.

Since the Duke and Duchess of Sussex first took Archie across the Atlantic, he has been adapting to his new environment, climate and circumstances. Public access to him is restricted, as it should be; but his parents make occasional concessions to the ongoing public interest in him and his progress. Since leaving the UK they have shared stories and occasional pictures of him on their Instagram page; and they released a new photograph of him in December 2019 to mark the end of the year.

In the photo, Prince Harry is seen standing beside the sea holding his then seven-month-old son in his arms and grinning from ear to ear. It's not clear exactly where the shot was taken but the Sussexes are said to have spent the festive period on Vancouver Island, off the coast of West Canada and this looks to be the most likely location. Both father and son are wrapped up in warm clothing, with Harry wearing a khaki outdoor jacket and beanie hat while Archie is dressed in a brown coat, boots and an adorable knitted hat with a bobble on either side, which melted the hearts of observers across the world.

The Sussexes revealed that Archie seemed to love the cold winter weather across the pond. In January this year, Harry mentioned this when he spoke at a fundraiser for his charity Sentebale. "It has been a privilege to meet so many of you, and to feel your excitement for our son Archie," he said, "who saw snow for the first time the other day and thought it was bloody brilliant!"

Top left and above: Archie's first year began with an eagerly anticipated introduction to the world

"Privately, the 93-year-old monarch is said to have told Harry that she hoped Archie would still spend time with the Royal Family"

*Above and opposite: Baby Sussex
is granted a private audience with
Archbishop Tutu*

In addition to their charming wintry portrait, Harry and Meghan's Instagram post included a slideshow of images with Coldplay's "Clocks" playing in the background. It featured various 2019 highlights for the couple, together and solo, including Meghan's guest-edited September issue of British *Vogue*, Harry giving a heartfelt speech at the WellChild Awards in October last year and the couple's royal tour of South Africa later the same month.

The video caption read:, "Wishing you all a very Happy New Year and thanking you for your continued support! We've loved meeting so many of you from around the world and can't wait to meet many more of you next year. We hope 2020 brings each of you health and continued happiness."

A few weeks later, on 20 January this year, the world got another glimpse of Archie. This time it was courtesy of the paparazzi, who spotted Meghan taking her dogs for a stroll in Horth Hill Regional Park in Victoria, near the ocean-front mansion on Vancouver Island where she and Harry had spent Christmas. With two police bodyguards walking behind her, the duchess wore casual clothes and a relaxed smile as the lensmen took their shots. Archie's features were not visible this time, as he was facing his mother and snuggled in a sling.

Meghan had her hands full in the pictures. Holding two leads in one hand, she was trying to steer her black labrador Oz and beagle Guy in the same direction while keeping a protective and stabilising arm round the eight-month-old bundle on her chest. As the dogs meandered along veering right and left, Meghan struggled to keep them on course and the straps of the baby carrier in place on her shoulder.

A few weeks after these sightings of Meghan, the Canadian government revealed that officers from the Royal Mounted Police would no longer guard the Sussexes when the transition period ended on 31 March. Scotland Yard also came under increased pressure about the huge

Harry and Meghan visit the Auwal Mosque in Cape Town on their tour of South Africa, September 2019

cost of protecting the couple, given that it had been their decision to quit their roles as senior royals. Should they still be entitled to round-the-clock armed protection from specialist officers? Public opinion thought not.

The late Princess Diana's former bodyguard, Inspector Ken Wharfe, warned that the Queen's great-grandson Archie was at "real risk" of being kidnapped, and that therefore Her Majesty should be the one to pay for his family's security. A personal protection officer is thought to cost around £100,000 a year, and Harry, Meghan and Archie would need two each. Then there would be accommodation, travel and administration costs on top. Wharfe, appearing on Good Morning Britain, said he believed these figures were accurate.

Asked about Archie's protection, Wharfe said, "He's part of the package. It doesn't matter if he stays in Canada or comes to the United Kingdom, the building they are staying in has to be secured even when they are not there." Wharfe flagged up one of the central problems arising from Harry and Meghan's new status as non-royals. "Freedom," he said, "comes at a cost."

The couple set off on 9 March to start their new life in North America after attending the annual Commonwealth Day service at Westminster Abbey, where the Queen led the

"Our son Archie saw snow for the first time the other day and thought it was bloody brilliant!"

congregation. It was the final act in their capacity as senior royals, although many believe the Queen's agreement with the couple leaves the door open for them to return to the fold if they ever change their minds.

On British Mother's Day, 22 March, the Sussexes posted their own online greetings card on Instagram, a simple eight words on a dark blue background: "Mummy. Mum. Mom. Mama. Granny. Nana. Thank you." The caption alongside it read, "No matter what you call your mum, this Mother's Day in the UK, we honour the mums all over the world who do so much every single day, and now more than ever." The American equivalent falls on 10 May, four days after Archie's first birthday. It will be Meghan's second US Mother's Day. To mark her first, when Archie was just a few days old, the Sussexes posted an image on Instagram. It was a cute close-up of Archie's bare baby feet, exposed to the warm outdoor air and supported by his mother's hand.

The next baby photo to be posted on the Sussexes' Instagram page was on 16 June 2019, Father's Day. This one showed Archie gazing at his father and grasping his middle finger in his tiny hand. There was no further sign of him until 15 September, Harry's 35th birthday. A christening photo showed master Archie in the traditional ceremonial gown, lying in his mother's lap with his adoring father leaning over him. It was one of nine

Opposite: The Sussexes meet Graça Machel, widow of the late Nelson Mandela, October 2019

Below: Harry gives a speech at a fundraiser for his charity Sentebale, January 2020

Opposite: Meghan joins pupils at a London school on International Women's Day, March 2020

images posted together with a birthday message from Meghan. Each photo – including a classic one from their May 2018 royal wedding – represented a different chapter in Harry's life so far.

On 31 March 2020 the Sussexes stopped updating their SussexRoyal website or the accompanying Instagram feed, so ending the regular updates. Quite by coincidence, it was around the time that much of the world entered lockdown in response to the Coronavirus. By 6 May, like the rest of the world, the Sussexes were under lockdown as they celebrated Archie's first birthday. From their accommodation in Los Angeles, they released a video for the website of the British charity Save The Children, inviting viewers to donate. Harry recorded Meghan reading Archie a picture book entitled *Duck! Rabbit!*, written by Amy Krouse Rosenthal and illustrated by Tom Lichtenheld. According to some accounts, the doting parents celebrated Archie's birthday by enjoying Zoom calls with friends and family around the world, while *People* magazine speculated that the duke and duchess may have treated Archie to a "smash cake" – a giant cake that a toddler is encouraged to tear apart. However the family chose to celebrate the first birthday of Master Archie Harrison Mountbatten-Windsor, we can all wish him many happy returns and a healthy, fulfilling, normal-as-possible life ahead.

The Duke and Duchess of Sussex
weather the storm at the Endeavour
Fund Awards, March 2020

A bolt from the blue

Harry and Meghan's shock New Year announcement forced the Royal Family to make new moves towards modernity

It was on a cold February day back in 2018 that Prince Harry greeted hundreds of people lining the road up to Edinburgh Castle. They had gathered there to wish him well ahead of his wedding that coming May to the American actress Meghan Markle. The prince and his bride-to-be shook hands with the crowd and exchanged pleasantries. The vibe was upbeat, despite the biting cold. Children could hardly contain their excitement at meeting the beautiful Meghan, while Harry jokingly told one woman in the crowd she had the warmest hands he had felt that day.

Fast forward two years to the end of February 2020. Harry was visiting the same city but this time he was on his own and the contrast in mood was quite marked. On this occasion it was all about goodbyes. And there was no enthusiastic throng waiting to welcome the Queen's third grandson.

It had been a tough few months for the Royal Family. In early January, Harry and Meghan had dropped the bombshell – without warning – that they intended to step back as senior royals. Since then they had been locked in urgent discussions with the Queen, Prince Charles, Prince William and high-ranking courtiers.

"We intend to step back as 'senior' members of the Royal Family and work to become financially independent while continuing to fully support Her Majesty The Queen," read their somewhat earth-shattering statement. "It is with your encouragement, particularly over the last few years, that we feel prepared to make this adjustment. We now plan to balance our time between the United Kingdom and North America, continuing to honour our duty to The Queen, the Commonwealth, and our patronages."

The manner in which the statement was released was perceived to have infuriated the senior royals. After being briefed, the BBC reported that, "no other member of the Royal Family was consulted before Harry and Meghan issued their personal statement." BBC royal correspondent Johnny Dymond said, "The Palace is understood to be 'disappointed'," a word that dramatically underplayed the significance of the situation.

The Sussexes' statement itself raised complex questions, from taxpayers' support for the royals to the future of the monarchy itself. But their desire to step back was not new. The couple explained later that there had been "many months of reflection and internal discussions".

Still, the statement left Buckingham Palace reeling, especially as there was no consultation with the Queen or Prince Charles before it was released. It was thought that the couple had gone ahead in this way to force the monarch's hand. If they hadn't, secret discussions may still have been ongoing.

As it turned out, Harry had originally contacted Prince Charles just before Christmas about spending more time in Canada and the United States. He then asked for a meeting with the Queen at Sandringham. She agreed; but it was reportedly blocked by palace courtiers. The Queen asked Harry not to go public but he and Meghan did just that, blindsiding the entire family with their sudden announcement.

The Queen was said to be "hurt" and it was rumoured that the Duke and Duchess of Cambridge were furious. The Prince of Wales was thought to be very distressed by what this would mean for his future dream of a "slimmed-down monarchy", in which he saw the Duke and Duchess of Sussex playing a large part.

An emergency, top-secret royal summit was held at Sandringham on 13 January. It was hosted by the Queen and led by Prince Charles, with Prince William and Harry in attendance. Meghan, who had already returned to Vancouver Island to be with Archie, was initially expected to take part via a conference call. But in the end it was decided this would not be necessary. Harry would presumably represent her in expressing their joint intentions.

The Queen afterwards issued a statement saying they had had "very constructive discussions on the future". She said she respected and understood the Sussexes' wish to live a more independent life. She also said that they had made it clear they did not want to be reliant on public funds in their new lives; and that there would be a "period of transition" in which the Sussexes would spend time in both Canada and the UK.

On 18 January the Queen released a statement saying she had thrashed out an "agreement" with Harry and Meghan. "Following many months of conversations and more recent discussions, I am pleased that together we have found a constructive and supportive way forward for my grandson and his family. Harry, Meghan, and Archie will always be much-loved members of the family. I recognise the challenges they have experienced as a result of intense scrutiny over the last two years and support their wish for a more independent life. I want to thank them for all their dedicated work across this country, the

Commonwealth and beyond, and am particularly proud of how Meghan has so quickly become one of the family. It is my whole family's hope that today's agreement allows them to start building a happy and peaceful new life."

Details of the agreement were released. The major losses for Harry and Meghan were that they were to give up their royal duties, no longer receive public funds and pay the money spent on their Frogmore Cottage renovations back to the public purse. They would pay rent on the cottage and would no longer represent the Queen at home or abroad.

On 21 January, Harry returned to Vancouver Island, desperate to see his wife and son. A month later it emerged that the Queen could not allow Harry and Meghan to call their brand "Sussex Royal" as part of the deal was that they were no longer to be called "royal".

This was a huge disappointment to them because they had established the brand the previous year. Sussex Royal featured in the name of their official website and Instagram page, which carried a terse response from the couple on receiving the news. It said, "There is not any jurisdiction by The Monarchy or Cabinet Office over the use of the word 'Royal' overseas". Still, they reluctantly bowed to the Queen's request. They had both hoped for a new, self-financing, progressive, "half-in, half-out" role within the Royal Family; but as it turned out, this was not achievable.

Previous pages: A smiling Harry and Meghan step out at the Endeavour Fund Awards in London, March 2020

Below: The Queen announced a "constructive and supportive" agreement with the Sussexes

Opposite: The couple attend The Lion King European Premiere at Leicester Square, July 2019

"The Queen said she respected and understood the Sussexes' wish to live a more independent life"

The following week, on 26 February, Harry made his low-key appearance at Edinburgh Castle. It was the first date in an official farewell tour that would see the Duke and Duchess of Sussex, alone or together, winding up their public duties before the agreed 31 March cut-off point. The Sussexes' attendance at these UK events would be the last hurrah for the couple before they began their new life in North America.

Harry had arrived back in the UK alone on a commercial flight earlier that week and was spotted alighting from a London North Eastern Railway train at Edinburgh's Waverley station. He was travelling almost undercover, or at least not wanting to be spotted, and wore a baseball cap and jeans and carried his own bag. There was a police bodyguard present but no royal entourage fussing around him. Neither were there any flag-waving fans waiting outside the city's International Conference Centre. Harry had come to address an event organised by Travelyst, the sustainable tourism initiative he had launched with a group of major travel companies the previous year.

Inside the conference centre there was no fuss either. The prince had wanted it that way. Ahead of his short speech, event host Ayesha Hazarika told the gathering, "He's made it clear that we are all just to call him Harry." Some might have interpreted this to be a little dig at his family for denying him the right to use his HRH title. After all, he had been born a prince and the palace had made it clear he would always be one. But it seems more likely that this new informality was simply a reflection of how he saw himself going forward. He would now be judged, rightly or wrongly, in his own right and for his actions as a private person, not in the light of his heritage or royal pedigree. He would just be "Harry".

Left: the Duke of Sussex addresses a sustainable tourism summit in Edinburgh at which those present were asked "just to call him Harry", February 2020

In early March, Meghan arrived back in the UK without Archie, who had stayed behind for the Sussex's farewell tour. On 5 March she made a private visit, in her continuing role as patron of the National Theatre, to its Immersive Storytelling Studio. There, she learned about the use of virtual reality in developing new forms of emotive storytelling. Some photographs of the event were later released. A caption on the couples' Instagram page read, "The goal of this method of virtual reality is to enable us to better connect and empathise with each other as people, regardless of race, age or nationality." The photos showed the 38-year-old duchess dressed in white, with the musician Nubiya Brandon and her hologram, which both featured in the National Theatre's *All Kinds Of Limbo* exhibition.

That evening, the Sussexes made their first public appearance together since their shocking January announcement. The annual awards ceremony of the Endeavour Fund, of which Harry continues to be patron, is an occasion close to his heart. The March event, held at Mansion House, was to honour wounded service members who had taken part in sporting and adventure challenges over the past year. Numerous royal photographers turned out to witness the occasion. Many of them had been covering the official visit to Ireland of the Duke and Duchess of Cambridge but returned early to stake a claim to a place on the pavement and capture the first shots of Harry and Meghan's arrival.

The award-winning photographer Samir Hussein, son of veteran royal photojournalist Anwar Hussein, was very glad that he did. His portrait of the couple looked like an iconic movie still from a classic Hollywood romance. The pouring rain – despite leaving the snappers soaked – had lent a glistening glamour to his pictures, which were splashed all over the coverage the following day.

Hussein's photograph captured a perfect moment of shared love between Harry and Meghan, who smiled elatedly at each other. It was described as a snapshot of solidarity for a couple making a defiant return after an extended period of scrutiny.

The next day, Harry was driven to Silverstone by British Formula One racing legend and reigning world champion Lewis Hamilton. They arrived in style at the Northamptonshire racetrack in an electric Mercedes to open a new museum, the Silverstone Experience. This showcases the history of the championship Hamilton has won six times, and is the new home of the British Racing Drivers' Club Library and Archive. Harry was taken on a tour of the famous circuit.

On 7 March, the duke and duchess went together to the Royal Albert Hall for the Mountbatten Festival of Music. Harry appeared emotional when he and his wife received a standing ovation as they arrived and took their seats in the royal box. They both dressed in red regalia: the duke, immaculate in a Royal Marines officer's mess jacket while the duchess looked as glamorous as ever in a striking scarlet dress by London-based fashion label Safiyaa. The event was Harry's final engagement in his short-lived stewardship as Captain General of the Royal Marines – a role he took on when his grandfather Prince Philip relinquished it after almost 70 years. King George VI had also held and relished this public service role.

The final event the Duke and Duchess of Sussex attended was the annual Commonwealth Day service on 9 March, where the senior royals were also in attendance. But whereas the Queen was flanked in the front row by the Prince of Wales, the Duchess of Cornwall and the Duke and Duchess of Cambridge, the Sussexes sat in the row behind them.

Right: The duke and duchess meet band members at the Mountbatten Music Festival in London, March 2020

"Harry appeared emotional when he and his wife received a standing ovation as they arrived"

Opposite: Harry and Meghan arrive at Westminster Abbey to attend the Commonwealth Day Service, March 2020

If this sounds frosty, it didn't come across that way. In fact on 2 March, a week after Harry had returned to Britain, he had spent private time with the Queen at Sandringham. By then, tensions had reduced considerably. Harry's grandmother reportedly offered him and Meghan the chance to come back if they ever changed their minds about their new departure. She also extended an invitation to the couple and baby Archie to spend summer 2020 with her at Balmoral, her Scottish Highland retreat, which it is understood they have accepted.

At one of Harry's final speeches as a senior royal, during the Endeavour Fund awards ceremony, he looked close to tears as he made a barely veiled, heartfelt promise that he would "always" serve the Queen. In particular he addressed the current and former servicemen and women in the audience and spoke compassionately about the devastating impact leaving the military can have. "Being able to serve the Queen and country is something we're all rightly proud of," he said. "It never leaves us. Once served, always serving."

And when the couple's British visit was over, they were left in no doubt that they would always be welcome back.

Good enough to eat

Wooden Spoon Organic's beauty and babycare products are transforming the cosmetics industry

Wooden Spoon Organic's skincare products use natural, edible ingredients that are gluten-free and cruelty-free

"I don't want big problems," says Silviya Pavlova, managing partner and co-founder of Bulgaria-based Wooden Spoon Organic handmade skincare. "Big problems lead to big wrinkles. I want my company to be small and smart. I want to make products so pure that you can eat them for breakfast. I want to be an employer who invests in my staff's happiness. And I want to run a company that's so honest that it changes the values of the cosmetics business, and becomes a true example when it comes to environmental responsibility."

A savvy entrepreneur and mother, Pavlova's inspiration dates back to her student days, when the young Bulgarian travelled all over the world to countries as diverse as Mexico, Hong Kong, Vietnam, France and the USA. Pavlova noticed a common denominator among those destinations. "Every mother made skincare products and cosmetics for herself and her children with ingredients from her fridge."

Pavlova later joined a consumer goods company, but she was unhappy with the chemicals and animal testing involved in personal care products. "I remembered how those mothers in various countries used natural ingredients," she says. "And I spent three years trying to change the industry."

Eventually, Pavlova and her husband took stock. "He said, 'We're lucky; we can prioritise happiness.'" So she took a deep breath and quit her job. "At that time, I was making a wrinkle cream at home. I knew what to do, I knew where to go for ingredients – so, little by little, I developed my products. And one day, I was making serums in my kitchen for my girlfriends when my husband said, 'You should make this a business and sell them.' I laughed and said, 'What if nobody buys them?' He said, 'Well if that happens, we'll just call it an expensive hobby!'"

That was 2014. The couple opened a lab and pledged to produce honest, pure skincare products that meet the highest European standards. All Wooden Spoon body and babycare products are therefore gluten-free, cruelty-free and – with the exception of some beeswax – vegan.

"Our one-of-a-kind body butters are made fluffy without water and programmed to melt at skin touch," says Pavlova. "And our sunscreens are one of the few, if not the only ones in Europe, that offer a very high sun-protection factor using only five simple food ingredients. These are game-changing products."

Three months after launching, Wooden Spoon was selling in eight countries; it now sells in 36. "We're all about honesty," says Pavlova. "We make products for people who love the results and value pure ingredients. What's more is that, from day one, we have been focused on being zero-waste company; and we're proud that everything – from the ingredients to the packaging – is processed in Europe." Wooden Spoon is Soil Association Cosmos Organic certified, and tries hard to use as much biodegradable product as possible.

Pavlova is also dedicated to her largely female team. "I don't want anyone at Wooden Spoon to compromise either on work or parenthood – so we're the only company I know in Bulgaria where all the employees are home by 4pm every day. We're modern wives, mothers and professionals."

By staying small, says Pavlova, she can work flexibly. So while Wooden Spoon is growing and successful, its reputation has built up through word of mouth. And because Pavlova takes such pride in her products and presides over a happy team working flexible hours, she keeps her problems small – and her face wrinkle-free.

www.woodenspoon.eu

The unbelievable tooth

It sounds like one of Willy Wonka's fantasy confections, but Theodent toothpaste has discovered a chocolate extract that really does rebuild teeth better than fluoride

It sounds like a particularly far-fetched fantasy from *Charlie And The Chocolate Factory*, but the chocolate extract in Theodent toothpastes actually rebuilds our teeth by regenerating, hardening and strengthening the hydroxyapatite in the enamel.

The story begins in the 1980s when two Louisiana-based medical practitioners – Dr Malektaj Yazdani and Dr Tetsuo Nakamoto – received a grant to study the harmful effects of caffeine consumption during pregnancy and its effect on the newborn. Dr Arman Sadeghpour, son of Dr Yazdani and mentee of Dr Nakamoto, was sent as young boy to conduct research in Nakamoto's lab at the Louisiana State University Health Sciences Center.

"We found a compound in chocolate that works better than fluoride to remineralise tooth enamel," says Dr Sadeghpour. "Dr Nakamoto, Dr Simmons and Alexander Falster collaborated on the early caffeine research, looking at variant molecules that are similar in structure to caffeine, thinking that these would also be harmful. In so doing we ultimately formulated and trademarked Rennou – a potent extract from cocoa. We were amazed and delighted to find it had the totally opposite effect of caffeine. It actually regenerated, hardened and strengthened the enamel."

The team soon founded the company Theodent LLC in New Orleans with co-founder Joseph Fuselier. Since 2012, it has brought three products to market: a daily adult toothpaste (Theodent Classic), a clinical-strength product (Theodent 300), and a safe-if-swallowed chocolate-flavoured children's toothpaste (Theodent Kids). All are fluoride-free and able to regenerate and strengthen the minerals in teeth and bone. "In terms of regrowing enamel," says Dr Sadeghpour, "it's truly magical."

In fact, according to an 80-patient double-blind clinical trial conducted at the University of Texas Health Science Centre in San Antonio in 2014, Theodent beat Colgate and Prescription Sensodyne on all four measurements affecting sensitivity, due to its incredible enamel-rebuilding capacity. And, according to a 2013 study, Rennou is actually 71 times more potent than fluoride in its effects and is not harmful if swallowed. "Our regular adult toothpaste beats even prescription toothpastes in repairing and reversing cavities in their early stages," says Dr Tetsuo Nakamoto, Chief Scientific Officer. Even more astounding, when it came to regenerating tooth enamel, the trial showed a 100 per cent patient success rate in just three days.

Theodent's commitment to producing vegan fluoride-free toothpaste reflects the values of modern parents like Harry and Meghan. "Theodent toothpaste offers an alternative to fluoride that's more effective with no toxicity," Dr Sadeghpour explains. "Other toothpaste brands aren't really responding to global trends for ethical, natural products, particularly when it comes to the active ingredient. Fluoride toothpaste isn't good enough or even ethical anymore, particularly for kids. Humankind deserves better."

The product has an undeniably universal appeal. "Everyone struggles with dental decay," says co-founder Joseph Fuselier. "It is the only disease that every single human being on the planet suffers from."

Theodent is sold in the USA and Canada, Russia, the Middle East, China and Hong Kong. It's also available in Britain from Harrods, Selfridges, Whole Foods and other outlets – including the Wigmore Street pharmacy John Bell & Croyden, which bears a Royal Warrant.

Ultimately, Dr Sadeghpour is keen to see the health benefits of chocolate appreciated as universally as its flavour. "We're passionate about the difference we can make," he says, "and we hope to ultimately replace fluoride in the worldwide oral-care market. So dream big, kids."

www.theodent.com

Theodent's products include toothpastes that help to remineralise tooth enamel

Wrapper's delight

FabRap's beautiful printed fabric squares that serve as an eco-friendly, reusable alternative to wrapping paper

FabRap uses ethically sourced cotton to make bold and beautiful present wrapping

"The act of giving is such a powerful way to communicate our love for a person, so the presentation of the gift is very important," says Hema Kumar. "I offer something that is a beautiful, reusable alternative to paper." Hema is the founder of FabRap, whose printed fabric squares are an innovative, highly attractive and sustainable way to wrap gifts.

The excitement of tearing the wrapping paper from a present is a universal experience, but one that sits uncomfortably with the waste it produces – around 50,000 trees are felled annually in the UK simply for Christmas paper. FabRap's cotton squares, which can be neatly folded and tied around a gift, recall the ancient Japanese tradition of furoshiki. "It is a lot faster and easier to wrap with fabric as it doesn't rip," says Hema. "If you make a mistake you can untie it and start again." Using FabRap's double-sided fabrics adds a contrasting flash of colour to the knot fastening.

Although a simple concept, Hema spent years developing FabRap to ensure that the company had solid ethical foundations before she launched it in 2018. She uses 100 per cent Global Organic Textile Standard (GOTS) certified cotton, sourced in India. "I wanted to support Indian farmers who made the decision to move to organic production," she says. "It's important to make sure the people who make your product receive the right pay, holidays and working conditions – that takes time, but I am really committed to it."

The designs, also printed in India, are unique to FabRap. "The patterns need to be timeless, though contemporary, as the fabric will be used over and over again," says Hema, who has made short how-to films showing how to wrap even awkward shapes quickly and securely. As a female entrepreneur, she is keenly aware of making sustainable choices as her brand grows and plans to work with community-led manufacturers in rural India, adding new prints, colours and product sizes to the range.

"It is important that people have an alternative to paper that they are proud of giving and receiving," she says. "I get incredible comments about FabRap because it enhances the joy of giving and people appreciate that they can keep and re-use the fabric." *www.fabrap.co*

Wooden it be nice

Wiwiurka handcrafts adventurous wooden play furniture, with each item performing a pedagogical function for children

Wiwiurka's brightly coloured children's furniture is made by local artisans using sustainable wood

I f you were looking for the definition of "family business" you couldn't find one much better than Wiwiurka. This Mexican company creates an imaginative and playful range of brightly coloured, handmade children's furniture that addresses the needs of kids and parents alike, elevating play while offering aesthetic designs. Each item is created by husband-and-wife team Marek and Ana, and tested by their three daughters before it hits the shelves. "Marek and Ana started this line of products after the birth of their first daughter," says customer service team member Ines Carmona. "When searching for this sort of furniture, they realised it would be easier to make the items than find them elsewhere."

The journey began when Marek moved to Mexico from Germany. As a tree surgeon, he had started to fashion offcuts of wood into playground equipment. This soon evolved into the concept of Wiwiurka, which takes the playground into the home with a series of wooden items that are inspired by, and named after, the pedagogical approaches to children's development of education pioneers Pikler, Montessori and Waldorf. Wiwiurka – named after the Polish word for squirrel – makes cool, colourful rockers and climbing frames, fun indoor swings, ramps and slides, indoor and outdoor trapezes, small toys and rope ladders, all handmade from fine wood and perfectly finished.

"Everything is aimed towards creative, free play," says Carmona. "The idea is to reach kids' imagination and encourage them to exercise at home, so they don't always need to go to the park. It gives parents a nice indoor-play option while boosting kids' motor skills."

Wiwiurka currently sells 80 per cent of its products internationally and is now obtaining the necessary certification for the US and European markets. The furniture is all carefully made by local artisans using sustainable pine and plywood wherever possible and the vibrant paints are non-toxic and chemical free. "This is a workshop full of attention to detail," says Carmona. "Each piece is carefully cut and sanded with a lot of care and love. Our people know that these items will end up in somebody's home to make kids happy, so they love what they do. There is a lot of love in the creation of our items."
www.wiwiurkatoys.com

Walking
the walk

Meghan looks set to continue
what she has always done to
model a sustainable lifestyle

In the same way that the Duchess of Cambridge triggers "the Kate effect" whenever she wears anything identified as a high-street or online brand, Meghan causes a corresponding stir over her fashion choices. Except, if anything, the Meghan Effect works even faster. Where an item that Kate has worn in public will sell out in a matter of hours, garments Meghan has been seen in can vanish from stockists in minutes.

It follows, then, that Meghan, the most ethically aware duchess ever, would use her clothing as a subtle message to promote sustainability. She knows that the scrutiny of her wardrobe can be good for those brands she admires that are also environmentally friendly, especially if they employ ethical production practices.

When the Sussexes toured Australia in October 2018, Meghan made a point of wearing ethically sourced clothes. Her outfits for that trip included items from Outland Denim, shoes from Rothy's and Veja and jewellery by Ecksand. Outland Denim employs seamstresses rescued from human trafficking and sexual exploitation. Rothy's flats are made entirely from recycled plastic water bottles, while Veja sneakers use recycled polyester, organic cotton and wild rubber. All of Canadian jeweller Ecksand's pieces are ethically sourced.

Above: Meghan wears a Staud dress made of recycled nylon during a trip to a mosque in Cape Town, September 2019

Opposite, top: The duchess wears Outland Denim on arrival at Dubbo Airport, Australia, October 2018

Opposite, bottom: Meghan in a dress by Malawian fair-trade brand Mayamiko during the Sussexes' visit to South Africa

James Bartle, founder of the Australian-based Outland Denim confirmed that Meghan's choices were completely intentional. "The Duchess's advocacy of human rights and the environment is evident in the brands she chooses to wear," he said. "It's clear she holds a preference for brands with substance, whose foundations are built upon respect for people and the planet."

On the royal tour of South Africa, Meghan wore several garments by international brands with a focus on sustainability. These included a belted shirt-dress from Room 502 (which uses ethically sourced materials, production and labour); a Staud dress made from recycled nylon; and a black-and-white dress from Malawian fair-trade brand Mayamiko. This time her wardrobe cost a fraction of what it had for the Sussexes' tour of the South Pacific.

On an everyday basis, Meghan is clearly an ethical fashion tastemaker, sporting anything from established labels like Stella McCartney and Gabriela Hearst to newcomers like British handbag brand DeMellier and Welsh denim manufacturer Huit. Hearst has always

promoted low-impact production; while DeMellier's A Bag, A Life initiative pledges that, with every bag sold, it will fund a set of vaccines aimed at saving the life of a child.

Meghan's environmental principles sit comfortably with the long-term goals of her father-in-law, the Prince of Wales. Of all Prince Charles's many concerns, his commitment to environmentalism, sustainability and ethical trade is one that has been enthusiastically embraced by the younger royals. In a 2018 speech, Prince Harry joined the International Sustainability Unit to lend support to his father's campaign to raise awareness of the plight of the world's coral reefs. One of Meghan's first royal roles was patron of the animal welfare charity Mayhew.

The Duke and Duchess of Sussex have also supported the Prince of Wales's promotion of ethically sourced fabric, in particular wool, while Meghan's writing has consistently supported Prince Charles's interest in organic food and sustainable farming. The latter was reflected in Harry and Meghan's choice of wedding cake for their nuptials, when they commissioned the Hackney-based baker Claire Ptak – a champion of ethically sourced, healthy ingredients – to make it.

"Meghan has used her clothing as a subtle message to promote sustainability"

Left: Claire Ptak, the ethical baker who created Harry and Meghan's wedding cake

Opposite: Meghan sports Rothy's flat shoes on the beach in Australia, October 2018

Left: Harry and Meghan included several sustainable elements to the renovations of Frogmore Cottage

The couple have also explored other eco-friendly options in their time together. When renovating Frogmore Cottage, for instance, they used vegan, cruelty-free paints from the Organic & Natural Paint Company's Auro line, and installed a energy-efficient boiler. Meghan also made sure that Frogmore Cottage had an organic plot of land for growing herbs and vegetables, something she has done from a young age and something she aims to have for any house she stays in.

Indeed, it looks likely that Meghan will continue to explore the lifestyle that she herself wrote about on her now-defunct website, TheTig.com, in April 2016. Among many articles on sustainability, organic food and environmentalism were a series of tips from a female-run media company Our Name Is Farm. The article recommended signing up for Community Supported Agriculture, shopping at local farmers' markets, reducing waste by using all the scraps, and shopping local wherever possible – all tips that Meghan and Harry have doubtless been employing while in lockdown. "It's important," wrote Meghan, "that we never forget the wellbeing of our good ol' Mama Earth."

A climate of change

Harry, like Meghan, has long been using his influence
to raise awareness of environmental issues

Like many other members of his family, Harry has a long history of promoting environmental awareness. It is a topic that unites both Harry and Meghan and has become a prime focus of concern for the couple. Their travels around the world have led both to witness the dire ecological problems faced by the planet and the need for urgent and immediate conservation efforts. "The call to protect our environment is more urgent now than at any other time in human history," they announced on their SussexRoyal website. "Supported by overwhelming scientific evidence, our earth and seas are warming, and temperatures continue to rise. Our natural resources and critical ecosystems are facing unprecedented, and in some cases, permanent destruction."

It's something that Harry elaborated upon in a passionate essay published in the *Sunday Telegraph* in September 2019. "Conservation used to be a specialist area, driven by science," he wrote. "But now it is fundamental to our survival and we must overcome greed, apathy and selfishness if we are to make real progress." This was not some crank belief, to be dismissed as the province of "hippies", says Harry. It was about maintaining a balance between humans and the natural world to guarantee the survival of the planet. "Humans and animals and their habitats fundamentally

need to co-exist or within the next 10 years our problems across the globe will become even more unmanageable."

Many of these points chime with the values espoused by his father. Prince Charles's 2010 book *Harmony: A New Way Of Looking At The World* sees him link his views on the environment with ideas about religion, architecture, education and medicine in an overarching philosophy that he describes not as holistic but as "whole-istic". Harry would agree with many of the Prince Of Wales's conclusions, although he appears to have subtracted many of the more eccentric cultural ideas from his father's narrative. Where Charles's opinions on the environment are sometimes muddled by his controversial views on alternative medicine, for instance, Harry stays on topic, dealing very pragmatically with environmental issues, and trying to find real-life ways of addressing these issues.

The Duke of Sussex's understanding of these issues appear to have become deeper in the last decade. He credits much of this learning to his visits to Southern Africa, where he has dedicated much of his time to learning from researchers, guides and veterinarians who are all experts in their fields. After completing a decade in the military in 2015, Harry spent three months exploring the conservation sector in South Africa,

> # "Conservation is fundamental to our survival and we must overcome greed, apathy and selfishness if we are to make real progress"

Left: Harry with the bones of a rhino killed for its horn in Kruger National Park, South Africa, December 2015

Lesotho, Namibia, Tanzania and Botswana. He became particularly interested in frontline conservation projects, be they anti-poaching patrols in the Kruger National Park, big cat preservation projects or environmental educational programmes. In 2017 he became a patron of Rhino Conservation Botswana and also became president of African Parks, a non-profit organisation which takes a direct responsibility for the rehabilitation and long-term management of protected areas, in partnership with regional governments and local communities.

One point he has emphasised is that environmentalism is not a top-down, patrician process that ignores local people – as has often been the perception in the past – but is instead about empowering local communities to safeguard and manage their natural assets. "We need to learn from our past mistakes and support and educate those who are responsible for protecting the very assets that they and we depend upon, and we have a responsibility to provide opportunities," he wrote in his *Telegraph* essay.

Eco-tourism was one of these key areas. "This sector is perhaps one of the greatest threats, but it can be one of the greatest opportunities to heal many of the world's problems," he says on the SussexRoyal website. "The tourism industry

generates nearly nine trillion dollars a year, creates one in 10 jobs worldwide, and will have serviced approximately 1.5 billion international trips in 2019 alone."

The *Telegraph* essay starts to explain how. "Based on what I've learnt over the years and the experts that I've met, one of the greatest opportunities to deliver this balance is eco-tourism, but specifically community-based eco-tourism," he wrote. "Tourism which allows the communities to be equal financial partners through mentorship, so that they can see the investment flow back to their families, providing jobs, healthcare and a future."

It is something that he and Meghan are planning to address with their global tourism initiative, Travalyst, a partnership with Booking.com, Skyscanner, Trip.com, TripAdvisor and Visa. Travalyst hopes to refocus the tourism industry and encourage it to voluntarily become more eco-conscious. He sees the industry as being perfectly placed to refocus itself on the local community, and to connect with people and their land.

"We believe in the power and importance of travel and that we also have a shared responsibility to our planet and to each other," reads Travalyst's mission statement. "We want to be the driving force that paves a new way to travel, helping everyone explore our world in a way that protects both people and places, and secures a positive future for destinations and local communities for generations to come."

Opposite and below: Harry and
Meghan visit Abel Tasman National
Park in New Zealand to learn about
local conservation projects,
October 2018

Harry and Meghan enjoy the natural splendour of New Zealand's Redwoods Treewalk in Rotorua, October 2018

"We believe in the power and importance of travel and that we also have a shared responsibility to our planet and to each other"

One of Travalyst's initiatives is to have a scoring system to work out how eco-friendly their flights are and to offset carbon emissions and support local communities. The end goal is to create a scoring system across all participating platforms that will explain how sustainably minded their holiday is.

Speaking at the Travalyst launch in Amsterdam in September 2019, The Duke of Sussex readily admitted that royals like himself, with their sizeable carbon footprint, are culpable in this mess. "No one is perfect," he said. "We are all responsible for our own individual impact. The question is what we do to balance it out." He listed deforestation, loss of biodiversity, the excess of plastic in the ocean and poaching. "All of these problems can sometimes seem too big to fix," he acknowledged. Conservation fails unless you put people at the heart of the solution and for far too long, that hasn't been the case. I have no problem in admitting that we are all part of the problem in some way, but a lot of us simply aren't aware of the damage that is being caused."

The Duke of Sussex speaks at an event for the ethical travel initiative Travalyst, September 2019

The society couple

Harry's own battles with mental health and his experiences in the military have inspired the Sussexes to lead the way in improving societal well-being

On Harry and Meghan's website, a quote from Archbishop Desmond Tutu is prominently displayed. "Do your little bit of good where you are. It's those little bits of good put together that overwhelm the world." These are words that the Duke and Duchess of Sussex have taken to heart. For them, communities in all forms – of people, geographies, ethnicity, gender and varied socio-economic groups – have the power to effect change, to combat bias and to promote shared values. "The Duke and Duchess of Sussex recognise the unique perspectives through which different communities view the world," reads the website. "And though this is a time of unprecedented challenges and polarisation, our communities have the capability to deliver solutions that will build a better future for all."

Harry has been candid about his own struggles with mental health, referring to it as a "festering wound", and has become something of a figurehead for the mental-health movement. In 2017 he opened up about how he sought counselling at the age of 28, having tried to ignore these issues in the two decades that followed the death of his mother. Later that year Harry, along with the Duke and Duchess of Cambridge, spearheaded the Heads Together charity, which began a more positive and productive conversation about mental wellness within the UK and

helped raise vital funds for eight mental health charities. In January 2019 Harry revealed that he practised meditation each day to help fight depression, and he later talked about the links between physical and mental well-being at the 2019 London Marathon. He returned to the subject last year while on his tour of southern Africa. "I thought I was out of the woods and then suddenly it all came back," he told ITV's royal reporter Tom Bradbury in a documentary in October 2019. "I realised that this is something I have to manage. Part of this job, part of any job, means putting on a brave face and turning a cheek to a lot of stuff."

In January 2020, Harry's first public engagement since stepping down as a "senior royal" was at the draw for the 2021 Rugby League World Cup at Buckingham Palace, where he praised the sport for launching a "mental fitness charter" – a five-point mental health initiative implemented to educate players, officials and volunteers. In early 2020 it was reported that Harry had been working for more than a year and a half on a TV series on the subject of mental health. Co-created and executive produced with Oprah Winfrey, the series will be screened on AppleTV+ later in 2020 and aims to explore the stigmatisation of mental health and equip people from all backgrounds with the right information and tools to thrive.

From his own experiences, and through years of conversation with people who are grappling with their own mental-health challenges and recovering from various traumatic experiences, Harry has seen how much easier it is for people to heal and grow when they're surrounded by a supportive and connected community. "When individuals are met with acceptance instead of stigma, love instead of judgment, and inclusion instead of isolation, they can develop to their fullest potential no matter what their experience," the SussexRoyal website says. "Too often, the stigma attached to mental health prevents people who are struggling from seeking the support that they need. The Duke of Sussex firmly believes that the management of mental wellness and mental fitness is the answer to most of our problems."

During Harry's 10 years in the Armed Forces he witnessed the lengths to which service members can go in order to keep each other safe. Harry's service included two tours of duty in Afghanistan, where he witnessed first-hand some of the suffering of both the Armed Forces and the people they are tasked to protect. Since then he has highlighted the support that wounded and injured service personnel and veterans need through the rehabilitation process. He has also worked to bring wider public attention to some of the potential challenges that service veterans might face as they make the transition to civilian life, as well as the enormous contribution they make to society.

Throughout his service and in the years afterwards, Harry has seen in close contact that combat injuries might impose limitations they do not curb a person's bravery, ambition or sense of adventure. He has sought to promote meaningful physical activity as a pathway to healing, as he is continually amazed and inspired by the abilities of these individuals. The Endeavour Fund, which he established in

Previous pages: Harry attends the
draw for the 2021 Rugby League
World Cup at Buckingham Palace

Opposite and below: The duke
meets Heads Together runners
before the 2017 London Marathon

"The role of sport in improving societal well-being has been a constant in Harry's charitable endeavours"

Left: Harry talks with wheelchair basketball players during the launch of the Invictus Games in London, March 2014

Above: The Duke of Sussex laughs with competitors at the Invictus Games British team trials, January 2016

2012, provides opportunities for wounded, injured and sick service personnel to incorporate sport and exploration into their recovery process. With activities that include triathlons, adaptive surfing and climbing certification courses, the Endeavour Fund enables service members to rebuild both their physical and mental fitness, gain the confidence that could be lost, and to reconnect with loved ones and community once more.

After seeing members of the British Armed Forces compete in the Warrior Games in Colorado 2013, Harry was inspired to create and launch the Invictus Games. An international sporting event for wounded, injured and sick service members, both serving and veteran, as well as their families and a global audience. The Invictus Games use the power of sport to inspire recovery, support rehabilitation, and generate wider understanding and respect for all who serve their countries on a daily basis. The first Invictus Games were held at the Olympic Park in London in 2014, followed by Orlando (2016), Toronto (2017), and Sydney (2018). The next Invictus Games were initially due to be hosted in The Hague, Netherlands in May 2020 but – with the Coronavirus lockdown making these dates impossible – there are currently plans to reschedule this, possibly to May or June 2021. Harry takes an active role in planning and promoting this tournament, bringing greater visibility to the resilience and courage of those that wear the uniform, as well as their families and friends who have shared in their sacrifice and success.

The role of sport in improvising societal well-being has been a constant in Harry's charitable endeavours. He continues to support

Harry awards the winners of the April 2019 London Marathon, Kenyans Eliud Kipchoge and Brigid Kosgei

Left: Harry meets students during his visit to Nottingham Academy to mark World Mental Health Day, October 2019

such initiatives because he has seen the effect that sport can have on marginalised youth, military veterans, the disabled and many other people who seek a balance in their own mental fitness. He is a committed advocate of Made By Sport, a mammoth fundraising campaign to support grassroots sporting activities in the UK which he launched in June 2019 with Olympic gold medallists Anthony Joshua and Nicola Adams. "Made By Sport is about providing an opportunity to young people all over the country to be part of something," he said at the launch. "Something they might not be getting at home or within their own community, but the moment they walk through the doors of a sports club or a gym, they are part of a team – with purpose."

In 2014, Harry began volunteering in London's Personnel Recovery Unit, which supports wounded, injured, and sick service members in their healing process. During their time at Personnel Recovery Centres, service members receive comprehensive physical and mental health support – including medical care, skills training, personalised recovery plans, and community activities. He is deeply committed to advocating for these service members and honoured to have the chance to play a part in their recovery.

Another cause close to his heart is that of HIV/AIDS, which sees him carrying on his mother's legacy in this field. Harry visited Lesotho in southern Africa in 2003, where he met children who had been orphaned in the AIDS pandemic. Along with Prince Seeiso of Lesotho,

he co-founded the charity Sentebale (meaning "forget me not" in the country's native Sesotho language) to offer long-term support for organisations working with children affected by HIV/AIDS. Harry has also worked closely with the Welsh rugby union international Gareth Thomas, who spoke out in November 2019 about being HIV positive, and Harry has supported Gareth's work with the Terrence Higgins Trust.

Through local and global community action, progressive change can be achieved far quicker than ever before. In 2020, The Duke and Duchess of Sussex plan to shape their charitable entity to respond to these pressing needs. After carefully considering a number of foundation models, and having researched the incredible work of many well known and lesser known foundations, the duke and duchess are actively working to create something different – a charitable entity that will not only help complement these efforts, but also advance the solutions the world needs most. It shows how Harry is still governed by the words of his mother, Diana, Princess of Wales. "Carry out a random act of kindness, with no expectation of reward," she said, "safe in the knowledge that one day someone might do the same for you."

"Another cause close to Harry's heart is that of HIV/AIDS, which sees him carrying on his mother's legacy"

Prince Harry and Prince Seeiso of Lesotho join Coldplay on stage during the Sentebale Concert at Kensington Palace, June 2016

A voice for equality

As an actor, a royal and as an activist, Meghan has never been afraid to champion human rights and female self-empowerment

If you look on YouTube you will find Meghan Markle's first ever television appearance. It is 1993 and the 11-year-old Meghan is on the Nickelodeon show *Nick News with Linda Ellerbee* to register her annoyance at a TV advertisement for a washing-up liquid called Ivory Soap. The advert featured footage of dishes being scrubbed by a woman's hands – wearing a wedding ring, of course – accompanied by the gender-specific voiceover: "Women all over America are fighting greasy pots and pans". Meghan, along with her elementary-school classmates, wrote to women's rights lawyer Gloria Allred and the then First Lady Hillary Clinton to protest against this tagline, and Allred and Clinton apparently pledged their support. Months later Procter & Gamble, makers of the washing-up liquid, changed the product's tagline to: "People all over America are fighting greasy pots and pans."

Even at the age of 11, Meghan was an articulate and clear-headed spokesperson for her cause. "If you see something that you don't like or are offended by on television or another place, write letters and send them to the right place," she says on the broadcast. "You can really make a difference, for not just yourself but for other people."

Meghan speaks of this moment as the catalyst for understanding that one small voice can have one very large impact. It was an early display of a commitment to feminism and equal rights that has informed so much of her work ever since. Prior to becoming a member of the Royal Family, Meghan – using the celebrity status granted to her by her role in the hit TV series *Suits* – worked with several organisations which aim to uplift women's role in society. As she said in a blog post in 2015: "I've never wanted to be a lady who lunches – I've always wanted to be a woman who works. And this type of work is what feeds my soul and fuels my purpose."

In 2014, she toured Afghanistan and Spain with the United Service Organizations, a non-profit that entertains US troops around the world. She also became a counsellor for One Young World, an impact forum for young leaders around the world, giving them a platform to make great change for the future. She spoke at the charity's 2014 summit in Dublin, raising the topics of gender equality and modern-day slavery. She continued for work with One Young World at its global summit in Ottawa in 2016 (where she was pictured talking to the Canadian Prime Minister, Justin Trudeau) and again, as the Duchess of Sussex, in 2019 in London.

In 2015, Meghan joined Dove's Self-Esteem campaign for International Day of the Girl, to support programming for educators and schools to foster self-confidence in young women and teenage girls, with a focus on the influence of the digital community and social media. In the same year she started a long association with the United Nations. As UN Women's Advocate for Women's Political Participation and Leadership, she gave an inspiring speech on gender equality on International Women's Day 2015, one that was witnessed by the UN's Secretary General Ban Ki Moon. Meghan also publicly supported HeForShe, a solidarity campaign for the advancement of gender equality, initiated by the UN and fronted by UN Goodwill Ambassador Emma Watson.

In 2016, Meghan travelled to Rwanda as Global Ambassador for the human rights group World Vision, to meet female leaders at the parliamentary and grassroots level, including in government and at Gihembe refugee camp. She worked on a community project that enabled young girls to stay in school, noting that infrastructure is one reason why many girls didn't receive an education. "I think there's a misconception that access to clean water

Previous pages: The duchess delivers a speech at the launch of Smartworks, September 2019

Above: Meghan at a UN Women event promoting gender equality, March 2015

Opposite: Promoting self-esteem as a UN Women's advocate , October 2015

is just about clean drinking water," said Meghan. "Of course, it is. But it's so much more than that. Access to clean water in a community keeps young girls in school, because they aren't walking hours each day to source water for their families."

While on this trip to Rwanda, Meghan was struck by another element which was hindering young girls from continuing their education – the stigma surrounding menstrual health management (MHM). In 2017, she travelled to India to further explore this vital issue and worked closely with the Myna Mahila Foundation, a grassroots organisation founded by the Indian activist Suhani Jalota. It aims to combat the stigma around menstruation and empowers women living in slum communities to manufacture affordable sanitary products that they can sell, enabling their daughters to stay in school, while also creating microfinance initiatives. As the Duchess of Sussex described in an op-ed piece she wrote for Time magazine in 2017, "When we empower girls hungry for education, we cultivate women who are

emboldened to effect change within their communities and globally." The Myna Mahila Foundation is now a part of the umbrella of charities supported by the Queen's Commonwealth Trust.

There was also a feminist component to TheTig.com, the website and brand that Meghan set up in 2014 to cover topics such as food, beauty, fashion and travel, alongside thinkpieces about self-empowerment and dynamic, inspirational women. In this time she developed a large social network following, with 1.9 million people following her posts on Instagram and over 350,000 Twitter followers. But after three years, in April 2017, she took down the entire website in preparation for the announcement of her royal engagement – some of the political content and product endorsements were presumably not appropriate for a working royal.

Even after her marriage to Harry, Meghan continued to forge relationships with grassroots organisations in the UK. In early 2018, the Duchess of Sussex visited a small kitchen at the in west London that provided access for

those affected by the devastating June 2017 fire at Grenfell Tower to cook meals for their families. With many quiet visits over the course of the year, Meghan collaborated with the women to highlight their multicultural recipes in *Together, Our Community Cookbook*, published by Penguin Random House in September 2018. This international bestseller raised the funds to enable the kitchen to be available for use seven days a week, instead of two.

In the same spirit in 2019, Meghan became patron of Smartworks, an organisation which assists women from problematic backgrounds to enter the workforce. This small non-profit equips women with the clothing and training they need to excel at job interviews, and allows them to return for further support once they have secured employment. On one visit, The Duchess of Sussex noticed an absence of wardrobe essentials, and worked behind the scenes to convene four clothing retailers to create the The SmartSet capsule collection for Smartworks clients. This special edition collection, which launched in September 2019, utilised the 1:1 model which Meghan felt was vital for the consumer to actively be a part of each Smartworks woman's success story. For every item purchased, the same item was donated to a woman at Smartworks. The success of the sold-out collection has equipped the organisation with enough key essentials to dress their clients for one full year.

Opposite: Smartworks aims
to help unemployed women
regain their confidence in the
jobs market

Below: Meghan attends a panel
discussion on International
Women's Day, March 2019

Meghan and Harry enjoy their visit to the Mayanga township near Cape Town, September 2019

"I've never wanted to be a lady who lunches – I've always wanted to be a woman who works. And this type of work is what feeds my soul and fuels my purpose"

Above: The Duchess of Sussex meets female technology entrepreneurs in South Africa, September 2019

Above, right: Meghan attends a discussion on gender equality, October 2019

Also in 2019, Meghan served as a guest editor of British *Vogue*, alongside Edward Enninful, the magazine's Editor-in-Chief. The September 2019 edition, entitled Forces For Change, became the fastest selling issue in *Vogue*'s 104-year history, and the best-selling issue of the last decade. It featured 15 women on the cover, personally selected by Meghan and Enninful, each championing change in local communities and on a global scale. Readers were able to find articles of inspiration, inclusivity, female empowerment and fashion with purpose. "Forces for Change has proven to not simply be a moment, but rather a movement," says Enninful, who has dedicated a Forces For Change page to each monthly issue of British *Vogue* henceforth.

Meghan was an activist before she was a member of the Royal Family, and looks set to continue in this role as she and Harry start a state of semi-autonomy from the House of Windsor. In April 2020, the pair volunteered for Project Angel Food in their adopted home city of Los Angeles, delivering food for the city's residents who were unable to get out under lockdown. Similar initiatives are likely to play a role in Harry and Meghan's embryonic new charity Archewell (named after the Greek word "arche", meaning "source of action").

She may still be the Duchess of Sussex, but Meghan has always managed to combine her career as an actor and a royal with her humanitarian commitments. "While my life shifts from refugee camps to red carpets, I choose them both because these worlds can, in fact, co-exist," says Meghan. "And for me, they must."

The global stage

Harry and Meghan's affection for the Commonwealth
has always been clear for all to see

It had all began with such enthusiasm and promise. In an address to the Commonwealth Heads of Government meeting in April 2018, Prince Harry told the young delegates present that they were the future. It was his first speech as the Queen's new Commonwealth Youth Ambassador, a title Her Majesty had bestowed upon him. His pride in the role was evident for all to see.

Speaking at the Queen Elizabeth II Centre in London, Harry couldn't resist paying tribute to his then wife-to-be, Meghan, whom the Queen had made patron of the Association of Commonwealth Universities. "I am also incredibly grateful," he said, "that the woman I am about to marry, Meghan, will be joining me in this work, of which she too is hugely excited to take part in. In my new role I will work to support the Queen, my father the Prince of Wales and my brother William, all of whom know that young people are the answer to the challenges of today." He added that in performing the role, he would be drawing inspiration from his dutiful grandmother.

Fast forward two years and those hopes and dreams, expressed so eloquently, had been dashed by none other than Harry and Meghan themselves and their desire to carve out a new role for themselves. They had hoped to continue to serve the Commonwealth and the monarch, but their vision for the future was at odds with the

Queen's. Furthermore, relations between Harry and William, the brother he had promised to support, had become strained by the Sussexes' decision to step back from formal duties.

Not surprisingly, their invitation from the Queen to attend the Commonwealth Day service as their last appearance as senior royals is said to have mattered greatly to them. Although they will no longer formally represent the Queen or play as large a part in her beloved Commonwealth as she had planned, they will still be involved through charity work. And they remain president and vice president of the Queen's Commonwealth Trust, whose purpose is to "champion, fund and connect young leaders working hard to change the world".

Her Majesty's commitment to the Commonwealth is uncompromising. She has served as the head of the organisation all her life. Her passion and dedication to it is the same as it was on her 21st birthday when, in a radio address, she dedicated her life, "whether it be long or short" to the service of the people of the Commonwealth and "our great imperial family, to which we all belong".

Luckily, the Queen's life turned out to be long and, even at the great age of 94, her determination has not waned. On her arrival at Westminster Abbey she seemed undaunted by a long line of people to meet and greet and an even longer walk to her seat at the front of the building. She was joined in this procession by the Prince of Wales and the Duchess of Cornwall, who arrived at the Abbey just before her.

The younger royals had already rolled up according to their formal pecking order. The first to arrive were the Earl and Countess of Wessex. Then the Duke and Duchess of Sussex made their entrance to a very warm reception at the Abbey, and joined Edward and Sophie in the second row. The Duke and Duchess of Cambridge were next to arrive and took their places in front of Meghan and Harry. Charles and Camilla eventually joined them after processing with the monarch in full pomp and circumstance. They greeted the Sussexes amiably as they took their front-row seats. Meghan curtsied to Prince Charles and then to Her Majesty The Queen, the last to be seated at this public family reunion. She beamed at the assembled group, especially her beloved third grandson and his wife.

The 2,000-strong congregation that day included the prime minister Boris Johnson, Commonwealth secretary-general Baroness Scotland, high commissioners, ambassadors, faith leaders and more than 800 schoolchildren and young people. They listened attentively as the Queen gave her annual Commonwealth Day address, a transcript of which was printed in the day's order of service.

"On Commonwealth occasions," she said, "It is always inspiring to be reminded of the diversity of the people and countries that make up our worldwide family. We are made aware of the many associations and influences that combine through Commonwealth connection, helping us to imagine and deliver a common future." These words seemed all the more appropriate in light of the Windsors' inclusion of Meghan, the first "woman of colour", as she herself puts it, to marry into their clan.

Her Majesty highlighted how global connectivity makes people aware how their "choices and actions" could affect the "well-being of people and communities living far away", and educate them to be more careful with natural resources. This point touched on the issues around sustainability that increasingly preoccupy of the younger royals.

The heavyweight champion Anthony Joshua made a speech at the service, speaking movingly of his dual Nigerian/British citizenship and the benefits of belonging to the Commonwealth. Also performing in a diverse line-up were the singers Alexandra Burke and Craig David. All three were greeted warmly by the Sussexes after the event, highlighting what the Commonwealth stands to lose now that the firm's most fun couple is stepping down.

So there it was. The Sussexes had made their final royal appearance together with their inimitable combination of professionalism and panache. It caused

Previous pages: Harry and Meghan pictured with staff at Canada House, London, January 2020

Opposite and above: The duke and duchess on their tour of the Commonwealth in 2018

Below and opposite: Harry and Meghan take part in a roundtable discussion with the Queen's Commonwealth Trust at Windsor Castle, October 2019

onlookers and royal watchers to question the wisdom of their self-imposed exile, especially as they seemed to carry out their formal duties with such easy charm. They actually seemed to enjoy themselves and didn't give the impression of being on duty.

To many, Harry and Meghan seemed to have given up their senior roles too easily, without enough thought for the consequences both to themselves and to others. Ever since they undertook their first official Commonwealth visits to Australia, Fiji, Tonga and New Zealand in 2018 and to South Africa in 2019, they had been widely praised and promised so much.

And it was Meghan, even more than Harry, who had won plaudits for her slick performances on these royal tours. In 2018 at Fiji's University of the South Pacific, Meghan had been applauded for an impressive first speech about empowering young women through education. "Everyone should be afforded the opportunity to receive the education they want," she said, "but more importantly, the education they have the right to receive. And for women and girls in developing countries, this is vital." She was clearly emerging as a force for good and had a lot to give.

Indeed, what the Duchess of Sussex seemed to have in common with the Queen – other than her obvious love for Harry – was an interest in the Commonwealth. Meghan even made a point of underscoring her

commitment to it at her wedding to the prince. Witnesses to that almost unfeasibly perfect day in May 2018 will recall the duchess wearing a veil embroidered with flowers from each of the Commonwealth member nations.

So it was somehow fitting that Meghan's last day on official royal duties in the UK focused on not one, but two engagements linked to the global network. Not many people knew that on the morning of the Commonwealth Day service, the duchess performed her last official solo royal engagement.

Meghan had held a meeting at Buckingham Palace to discuss sustainability and climate change with a group of students from 11 Commonwealth countries. The event was off the record and details about it did not emerge until days later. But it seemed to sum up and promote the values we know Meghan holds dearest to her heart: education for all, global sustainability, and connecting with the Commonwealth.

The duchess presided over the meeting in her capacity as patron of the Association of Commonwealth Universities (ACU) and told the students, "Even though the groups are divided, everyone is connected because of this very holistic approach to tackling climate change. I love how solution-based you all are."

Halima Ali, a Kenyan lawyer researching energy and natural resources at Queen Mary University of London, talked positively about the involvement of the biracial duchess in the association so important to the Queen. "For Commonwealth and also African countries," she said, "to see her, her interest, her participation means a lot to us."

Above and opposite: Harry and Meghan at Westminster Abbey, March 2020

"Ever since they undertook their
first official Commonwealth
visits... they had been widely
praised and promised so much"

Above and opposite: This year's Commonwealth Day Service was the Sussexes' last appearance as senior royals

Joanna Newman, the Secretary General of the ACU, also had nothing but praise for Meghan. "We believe that higher education and universities are an essential part of nation building," she said, "and we want to build up healthy, strong, higher education systems across the Commonwealth and beyond. The duchess really understands that and she's a very powerful spokesperson for us."

Meghan herself was a scholarship student who graduated from Northwestern University with a double major in International Studies and Theatre. At the meeting, she met students supported by the Chevening scholarship programme, which grants international students access to postgraduate study in the UK.

Malawian student Timothy Biswick, who told Meghan about his work on tackling plastic pollution in the oceans, was impressed. "She knows what she's talking about in terms of climate change," he said. "She was talking about things in quite some detail so you knew this person knows what they are talking about and is passionate about it."

Meghan also discussed sustainable tourism, telling the scholars how she and Harry are only too aware of "the link between tourism and how much money is going outside of the country instead of [back into] communities." She described how, during the couple's first trip to Botswana early in their romance, she and Harry took off one night with just a backpack and a tent and camped under the stars.

In a video posted on the Sussexes' Instagram account, Meghan can be seen talking animatedly to the group and then listening carefully. At one moment, she seems to tell a joke and the students burst out laughing. She was clearly on sparkling form.

But she reportedly lost her characteristic composure after the students had left. Because then, all that remained for her to do then was say goodbye to the friendlier faces she had come to know in the gilded life she was leaving behind. It was as if the reality of giving up her royal status suddenly hit her – hard. It was all too much. She dissolved into tears.

Nonetheless, the duchess dried her eyes, changed into a stunning green Emilia Wickstead cape dress and, looking immaculate, accompanied Harry to the 2.15 Commonwealth Service at Westminster Abbey. The consummate professional, she seemed relaxed. It was as if she'd ordered a late breakfast and had all the time in the world to get ready.

When the Sussexes' triumphant swansong was over, the air was tinged with sadness as Meghan and Harry were whisked away in a car. She was taken straight to the airport to board a transatlantic flight home to the 10-month-old Archie. Harry followed a few days later.

Perhaps the Queen's Commonwealth message of diversity was ringing in their ears, filling them with a sense of missed opportunities. The day had been, as Meghan once said about her experience of adjusting to royal life and motherhood, "a lot".

But the authenticity of the couple's success as a double act is something the Sussexes are prepared to bank on in carving out an alternative future together. And we wish them the best of luck.

"They had hoped to continue to serve the Commonwealth and the monarch, but their vision for the future was at odds with the Queen's"

Right: Harry and Meghan meet schoolchildren at the Commonwealth Day Service, March 2020

Community champions

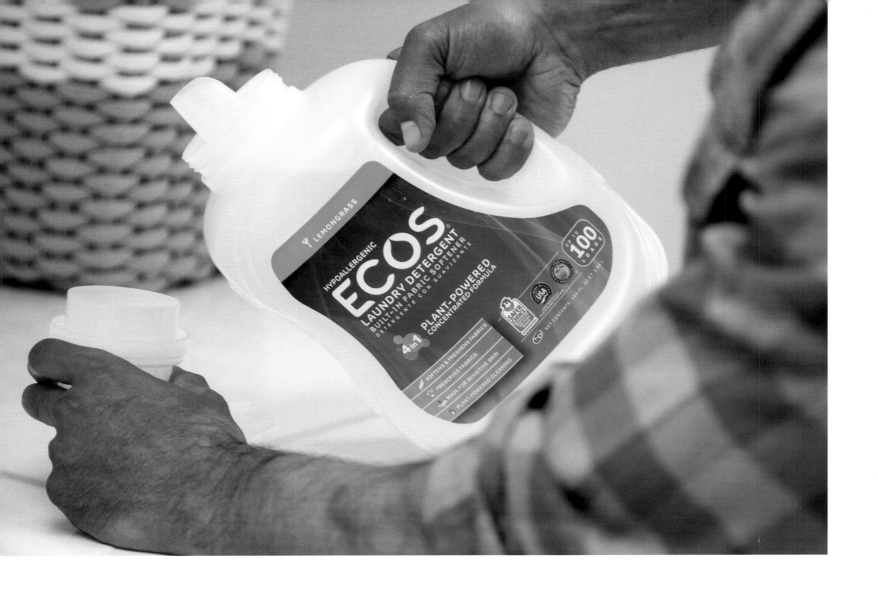

Clean and green

ECOS cleaning products avoid potentially toxic chemicals by using eco-friendly ingredients

"As a mother, I'm keenly aware that creating a healthy home is hugely important when bringing a baby into the world," says Kelly Vlahakis-Hanks. "Our goal is to empower consumers by creating cleaning products that are safer for families." Vlahakis-Hanks is President and CEO of ECOS, whose plant-powered laundry detergent and household cleaners offer a high-quality, green and affordable solution to keeping clean without harsh chemicals. "Our mission, our vision, is to make products that are safer for people, pets and the planet."

"Skin is the largest organ in the body, so it is important that we don't have toxic residues around us or on our clothing or bedding, especially when we have babies," says Vlahakis-Hanks. "Harmful residues on dishes and baby bottles can be ingested, making it especially important to choose detergents with safer ingredients." Her commitment to using natural ingredients, such as coconut oil, is clearly displayed on ECOS's product labelling. "We always disclose our ingredients because we believe that the consumer has a right to know what they're bringing into their home," she says.

ECOS, based in California, is a pioneer in green cleaning products. For more than 50 years, the determination of this family business, now under the stewardship of second-generation CEO Kelly, to offer consumers an alternative to traditional cleaning products has seen it grow into an international business. Hypoallergenic laundry detergent, hand soap and baby bottle wash are among ECOS's plant-powered products that clean without leaving a residue that can cause irritation or harm the environment.

The story behind ECOS is so rich and inspiring that it was made into a film, A Green Story, in 2012. Founded by a Greek immigrant in 1967, ECOS – which means "home" in Greek – was ahead of its time in creating cleaning products made with safer ingredients. Although green products are now very much in the mainstream and have been recently embraced by major detergent brands, ECOS has been in the green cleaning business exclusively for more than 50 years. "The fact is, we've been doing this for a long time and it's the only thing we do," says Vlahakis-Hanks.

Making safer green products was only half the story for Vlahakis-Hanks when she joined the family business in 2003. Her ability to connect with both consumers and grocery outlets brought rapid expansion, but to be true to the ideals the company was founded on, expansion had to be sustainable.

Since becoming CEO in 2014, Vlahakis-Hanks and her sustainability team have worked to make ECOS a model for sustainable industry. Today, its manufacturing bases across the US are carbon neutral, water neutral and zero waste, using 100 per cent renewable energy. "These are major milestones," she says. "As a privately owned company making our products ourselves, rather than through a third-party contractor, we can make decisions for long-term value instead of short-term profit." For ECOS, creating value means investing in safer ingredients, sustainable manufacturing systems and its employees.

ECOS added manufacturing capabilities in Europe in 2018, and is set to build more sustainable manufacturing facilities around the globe, offering consumers locally made green cleaning products. "Good business means doing well for our planet," says Vlahakis-Hanks, "and that means doing well for our families. Our products are about protecting the health and wellness of children and parents as well." www.ecos.com

ECOS's plant-powered products clean without leaving a residue

Bringing beauty to life

InLight Beauty has sustained its ethical, positive credentials through moments of real adversity – and come out on top

Opposite: InLight Beauty's range is informed by naturopathy.

Below: Loredana and Mariano Spiezia, co-founders of InLight Beauty

"Behind any successful venture is an attribute I consider to be very feminine," says Loredana Spiezia, co-founder of organic skincare company Inlight Beauty. "It boils down to one simple word: care. Care for ourselves, care for what we do, care for people around the world. I try to bring that spirit into everything I do as a businesswoman, a mother, a partner, and as a positive person who believes that there is always a bright side to be found when you look for it."

And she should know. Her family's story started out as a romance but turned into a nightmare that tested them to the limits. Twenty-one years ago, Loredana and Mariano Spiezia took their three children on holiday to Cornwall for the first time. They fell in love with its lush green landscape, spectacular coastline and friendly people. When they returned to Sorrento, they packed up their world, relocated to the Cornish village of Manaccan – and a new era of skincare was born.

"Mariano, a medical doctor, had always been interested in homeopathy, herbalism and nature's alchemy," says Loredana. "So we started studying and mixing herbs and making organic, natural skincare products. Very few people were making potions like ours back then. Because of the sound, scientific knowledge behind our formulations, we soon became the first skincare brand in Britain certified as 100 per cent organic."

But not long after they set up in business, disaster struck. "One night in May 2004, our neighbour knocked on our door at three o'clock in the morning. Our laboratory, which was in a converted barn, was on fire. Mariano, the children and I stood and watched all our hard work disappear in smoke. Oddly enough, the first thing my daughter, Maria-Chiara, said was, 'Mummy, there must be a bright side.' In that moment the flames were the only bright things I could see. But, deep inside, I knew she was right: something good would arise from all those ashes."

The Spiezias, with help from the Italian homeopathic brand Cemon, started all over again and relaunched InLight Beauty in 2006. They were determined it should remain an artisanal company and they still make their products by hand in Cornwall. The 22-line range is sold online and through select outlets, including Fenwick's of Bond Street; and according to Dr Mariano Spiezia, "They all prove that only nature respects the nature of our skin." The Line Softener Intensive, for example, was primarily designed to repair scars but it works wonders on wrinkles and sun-damaged skin. Loredana points to clinical trials that resulted in visibly smoother facial lines within 28 days. "It was amazing to see that such results could be achieved with a 100 per cent organic product," she says, "with absolutely nothing artificial added."

The ethos behind InLight Beauty chimes with values espoused by the Sussex Royals, who are known for their commitment to environmental issues, sustainability and ethical production. InLight Beauty is channelling these values. "We use local and sustainable materials wherever we can," says Loredana, "and only the purest organic ingredients." Like Meghan Markle, who will continue to promote the things she feels strongly about, the Spiezias are fierce defenders of these causes. "Our products respect nature," says Loredana. "All we add is our expertise, love and passion – and we believe we should lead in this market as much as we believe in our ethos and our products." In short, the people behind InLight Beauty really do care.
inlightbeauty.co.uk

Buttered up

IUVO Skincare specialises in natural, organic and vegan products

iUVO Skincare mixes shea butter and natural oils as the base for body creams, cleansers and face masks that heal, nourish and lift the spirits

IUVO SKINCARE is proof that good things can come from adverse situations. The shea butter body cream that Edith Gabbidon developed and refined as she was undergoing treatment for breast cancer is now the core product of an extensive all-natural, organic and vegan range of wonderfully nurturing face and body creams, cleansers and face masks.

Gabbidon was 52 when she was diagnosed with cancer. "I had to face it and get on with it," she says, calmly. "I had chemotherapy and radiotherapy and my body was not in a good place. A kind friend gave me a pot of shea butter as my skin had become dry and blemished. The shea butter was fantastic on my skin."

With the encouragement of her husband, Gabbidon started experimenting in her kitchen with her own cream. "I wanted a natural product that was vegan, good for the skin and that perked you up as well," she says. "After three months of research and experimentation I'd developed a cream that did all that. It felt so satisfying to put on. From there, we perfected the formula for other people so they could share our experience."

She spent a year blending essential oils such as rosehip, jojoba and neem oil with shea butter. After rigorous testing and retesting it resulted in a luxurious, highly effective cream that clears up blemishes, nourishes and improves the appearance of the skin and lifts the spirits. "Today, our leading products are the face and body cream, shampoo and conditioning bar and our antiperspirant deodorant bar," says Gabbidon. "We are really pleased with all our products, as they are all very labour-intensive."

From the outset, Gabbidon insisted on using only organic ingredients sourced from fair-trade co-operatives. She also uses sustainable packaging – jars are glass, wrapping is paper or bamboo. These rigorous standards have been rewarded with benchmark Ecocert certification and partnership with a large French producer.

New product launches are planned, but already the iUVO Skincare range has grown from its early kitchen creation to encompass shower gel, perfume and lip balm. From adversity, Gabbidon has created gorgeous-to-use products that heal, nourish and actively lift the spirits. "Our aspirations are to become a household name," she says. "It's not just skincare, its self-care."
www.iuvoskincare.com

Scents and sensibility

The skincare oils from de Mamiel use natural scents that can counteract stress

Annee de Mamiel blends science, Chinese medicine, aromatherapy and holistic philosophy into small and perfectly packaged bottles of stress-relieving goodness. Her natural skincare range's proven healing qualities, potency and purity have won her awards, a devoted following and a two-year waiting list for a consultation. "What I do and why I do it comes out of my clinic and my practice," says de Mamiel. "It's about how we deal with stress and how it ages us. Stress affects us both at an emotional level and at a very physical level."

For instance, de Mamiel's Seasonal Oils demonstrate her ability to match intense plant distillations to the stresses that seasonal changes put on the skin: for spring, an oil that brightens and stimulates; a summer oil to soothe and moisturise; a mood-lifting oil for autumn and a hydrating, warming blend for winter.

The company was launched in 2013, achieving cult status and winning several awards, including a position in the *Vogue* 100 Beauty Hall of Fame in 2016. Each hand-mixed, organic product is the result of years of research combined with a spiritual sensitivity. "Our de Mamiel products are first and foremost about performance and science, but with spiritual elements," she says. "There is a lot of science behind vibrations and sound, so oils get music played through them 24 hours a day."

As well as being deeply beneficial to the skin, de Mamiel's products also have holistic properties. "Inhaling the products works to balance the nervous system," she says. "The essential oils are blended in a way that changes the chemistry of the limbic system when you smell them, affecting cortisol levels that ease long term chronic stress."

The choice of plant ingredients is rigorous. "I use 12 different types of lavender, for example," she says. "Each is grown in a different region, in different soil and climate so has a different chemistry. Some regions produce an oil which is good for immune response while others have properties better for sleep."

The company's Stress Response Serums bring together a lifetime of study into metabolic pathways, stress and cortisol. "The serums target where a person holds their stress and how it affects them," says de Mamiel. "It's about finding a way through that so they don't take their stress from one day to the next." Pure, potent, sweet-smelling relief indeed. *www.demamiel.com*

The hand-mixed, organic products of de Mamiel combine scientific research with spiritual sensitivity

APPENDICES

The Royal
Family album

Photographs of the royals as youngsters have always
provided a heartwarming and less formal insight into
the lives of Britain's first family

*Above: Lady Elizabeth Bowes-Lyon,
the future Queen Mother, pictured
on her second birthday, 1902*

*Opposite: A baby Princess
Elizabeth, the future Queen,
is cradled by her mother, 1926*

Baby Sussex

Opposite: Princess Elizabeth, pictured with her mother, 1926

Above: Prince Philip, pictured at the age of one, 1922

Right: Princesses Margaret and Elizabeth stroke a family pet, 1936

Above: A smiling Prince Charles waves to his mother on his second birthday, 1950

Opposite: A baby Princess Anne with her parents, pictured on the day of her christening, 1950

Appendices

Top: Elizabeth and Philip relax in the grounds of Clarence House with Charles and Anne, 1951

Left: The royals share a family moment at Balmoral Castle in Scotland, 1952

Opposite: The Queen and Prince Philip, pictured with Anne (age 10), Andrew (age 7 months) and Charles (age 11) in the grounds of Balmoral Castle, 1960

Appendices

Above: The Prince of Wales,
pictured with Prince William
at Kensington Palace, 1983

Below: A one-year-old Prince Harry in the playroom at Kensington Palace, 1985

Appendices

*Above: Princes William and Harry
at Kensington Palace, 1985*

*Right: A young Prince Harry plays
with his mother, 1986*

Appendices

Above: A curious Prince George,
pictured at the christening of his
sister, Princess Charlotte, 2015

Opposite: Princess Charlotte,
pictured with her mother on
Christmas Day 2019

Credits

St James's House
SJH Group
298 Regents Park Road
London N3 2SZ

+44 (0)20 8371 4000
publishing@stjamess.org
www.stjamess.org

Richard Freed, Chief Executive
richard.freed@stjamess.org

Stephen van der Merwe, Managing Director
stephen.vdm@stjamess.org

Richard Golbourne, Sales Director
r.golbourne@stjamess.org

Stephen Mitchell, Head of Editorial
stephen.mitchell@stjamess.org

John Lewis, Deputy Editor

Jochen Viegener, Designer

Photography

Alamy, Getty Images, Robert Jobson, Adriana Yankulova (pp. 134–5). Other images are the copyright of individual organisations.

About the publisher

SJH Group is a world-leading creative media group that delivers bespoke solutions for a global client base. Comprising five unique publishing companies – St James's House, Artifice Press, Black Dog Press, SJH Publishing and Cargo Media – the group embodies a diverse selection of industry-leading publishers with a wide range of expertise. From the Royal Family to art and architecture, luxury lifestyle to global business, each company within the group shares a core ethos of professionalism.

Today's high-end publishing companies frequently serve as strategic partners for organisations that understand the power of well-connected publishers to communicate key messages for awareness, education and diversity. To this end, our world-class strategists provide companies, governments and campaigning bodies with publishing, business and marketing expertise for entertaining, informing and engaging some of their most important audiences.

As a recognised global publisher with top-tier clients and relationships with major sales outlets, our publications provide our partners with a once-in-a-lifetime chance to create a tangible product that tells their story, defines their DNA and clearly differentiates them in the marketplace.

In a media landscape that is saturated with digital, broadcast and disposable print formats, our books command the attention and respect from readers and provide a timeless resource for decades to come. Our publications – as well as their associated promotional activities – also provide our partner organisations with a unique opportunity to strategically engage with journalists, clients, business partners, professionals, academics and industry bodies.

Our books are consistently well received by their intended readerships, and several have appeared in the Amazon Top 100 book chart. On average, our publishing group prints more than 300,000 books each year. This places us on the UK's top-ten list for media distribution, and makes us one of the country's most influential distributors of published content across a broad range of specialist subjects.

www.sjhgroup.com

Sponsor index

A special thank you to the following sponsor organisations, without whose support this publication would not have been possible